The Way to My Heart
An Anthology of
Food-Related Romance

EDITED BY KELLY ANN JACOBSON

WITH CONSULTING POETRY EDITING BY SARAH ANN WINN

Copyright © 2017 Kelly Ann Jacobson

All rights reserved.

ISBN: 1548429821
ISBN-13: 978-1548429829

CONTENTS

    Acknowledgements
    Introduction

1.	Blood Orange *by Rachel Voss*	3
2.	Fresh Mushrooms *by Anna Schoenbach*	5
3.	Stanley *by Misha Herwin*	6
4.	Sablés, the Sandy Cookies *by Lynn Hoffman*	14
5.	Bouillabaisse *by John C. Mannone*	15
6.	Stolen Love *by Miguel A. Rueda*	16
7.	Trolling the Unknown *by Dianna Henning*	23
8.	Seeing the Fork First Time *by Betsy Fogelman Tighe*	24
9.	Diving Girl's Dining Guide *by Peter Marcus*	25
10.	French Cooking *by Mary B. Moore*	26
11.	Off the Menu *by Paulene Turner*	27
12.	Man and Superwoman *by Eric Paul Shaffer*	35
13.	Craving *by Jo Angela Edwins*	37
14.	Cookie Man and the Six Box Lady *by Chris Rodriguez*	38
15.	The Rum Anniversary *by Emily O'Neill*	44
16.	Chicken Soup *by Lynn Hoffman*	46
17.	Tell Me Her Name *by Judy Swann*	47
18.	Forty-Five Years Married, and Still, He Cooks for Me *by Alice Morris*	50
19.	It's All in the Timing *by Lynn Abendroth*	51
20.	Haiku *by Joanie DiMartino*	55
21.	Haiku *by Joanie DiMartino*	56
22.	Rosemary Chicken *by Jessica Abughattas*	57
23.	A Pair of Merry Mollusks *by Terri Elders*	58
24.	The *Ball* Jar *by Mary Ellen Talley*	62
25.	Sweet Basil *by Cameron D. Garriepy*	63
26.	Red Wine *by Steve Cushman*	70
27.	Excess in Paris *by Gretchen Fletcher*	71
28.	Harry & David's Royale Riviera Pears *by Katherine Edgren*	72

29.	Slice of Life *by Julia Tagliere*	74
30.	The Decade Menu *by Teresa De La Cruz*	77
31.	On Baking, Relationships, Etc. *by Marta Ferguson*	78
32.	The Tagine *by Susan McGee Bailey*	79
33.	Tapas Bar *by Steve Bucher*	86
34.	A, Your Name is Anna *by Sheila Wellehan*	88
35.	Fried Clams with a Side of Onion Rings *by Lucia Cherciu*	89
36.	Weather Report *by Gretchen Fletcher*	90
37.	I Came from the Village of Painted Toenails, You Came from the Village of Shaving Cream *by Dianna Henning*	93
38.	Kitchen Note: Severe Seafood Allergy, Seat 2 *by Emily O'Neill*	94
39.	Man-Hands *by Autumn Konopka*	95
40.	Lemon *by Emily Weitzman*	97
41.	Exhibition Eater *by Brandon French*	99
42.	Aubade *by Katherine Anderson Howell*	103
43.	First Fall Frost *by Brenda Yates*	104
44.	Breakfast at Pompeii *by Susan J. Erickson*	106
45.	Note on the Refrigerator *by Sharon Lask Munson*	107
46.	Sweetness *by Caroline Bock*	108
47.	The Flavor of September *by Pamela Murray Winters*	110
48.	Mermaid in the Kitchen *by John C. Mannone*	111
49.	Mormon and Jew: A Romance in Food *by Felicia Rose*	112
50.	Melding *by Bryn Homuth*	117
	Contributor Biographies	118
	About the Editor	127

ACKNOWLEDGEMENTS

I owe so much to the following people for helping me with this book: Sarah Ann Winn, who helped me sort through the poetry submissions; Randon Noble, who gave me the title; and Josephine Yu, who judged the contest. Finally, thank you, as always, to the incredible writers who trusted me with their work.

INTRODUCTION

Those readers who have heard me talk about my anthology process at past launches know that deciding the next book's theme is not a long, ponderous procedure. Instead, I arrive at every book's launch having decided that I will never, in a million years, do another anthology.

And then, inevitably, I listen to the voices of my talented contributors reading their quirky poems and stories and decide right there, in my seat, that I should reconsider my pronouncement.

On the night of the *Candlesticks and Daggers: An Anthology of Mixed-Genre Mysteries* launch, the same thing happened. However, as I celebrated the publication of my fifth (*and last!* I told myself) anthology, I didn't even have a burst of inspiration for what to do next. Sure, there were genres I hadn't tried, but perhaps the five I'd already covered—science fiction, personal essays, poetry, mystery, and fantasy—were enough.

Then I went to the cashier at Upshur and mentioned, in passing, that I hadn't done a romance anthology yet. "But I can't think of a unique spin," I added. "I can't just do romance."

"How about food-related romance?" she said.

I paused.

I briefly envisioned the book.

I sighed.

Now, when I page through *The Way to My Heart*, I can't imagine never putting this book together. More than any other anthology in the past, the poetry and prose in this collection work together and cluster around similar themes, helped by the prompt of needing a central human relationship in addition to a food focus. Together, they form one cohesive whole.

I am incredibly proud of this little book we crafted together, and I hope you fall in love with it the way I have. Perhaps it will be my last anthology...but probably not.

Kelly Ann Jacobson
Editor

BLOOD ORANGE
by Rachel Voss

I want to get under
your fingernails—you *know*
the feeling. Pitted and peeling,
undressed by the thumb
and forefinger, lingering
at the navel. White fibers
like threads pulled
from lacy underthings.

Find me in the rind,
what's too often discarded
in favor of flesh, tiny cells
of juice like discrete tear drops
tattooed in corners of eyes.
Porous skin, imperfect intimacy
of a lover's face seen
at close distances.

No tart grapefruit, no sweet,
petite clementine, I. Fine.
What am I if not the exotic
opposite of an apple, manifested
difference, idiom
of my own?

Historically craved by sailors like sirens,
minds singing with fruit.
Once a delicacy, gift
for long winter nights.
At Christmastime, they stuff me
full of cloves, protector
of charms, perfumed pomander.
Divided and shared like good luck
in the new year, gold
somehow in abundance.

THE WAY TO MY HEART

The best of me bleeds red
when cut, cross section
of desire, sanguine
Mediterranean evening,
liquid fire.

FRESH MUSHROOMS
by Anna Schoenbach

Simple.
Mushrooms with butter and garlic.
Add little more butter, salt and pepper – not complicated at all.
That's all they have. That's all they need.

Delicious.
Soft-fleshed, that earthy taste,
All the sponginess cooked away.
The cooked mushroom tastes pure and vital.

Unattainable.
My first love didn't like mushrooms.
They were mine to take from her plate.
But she never was. She never will be.

Beautiful.
Sprigs of parsley add color to the mushrooms.
Just as golden hair glints in the sun.
It is evening. The parsley wilts in the pan.

Silent.
Take the pan from the fire, let the sizzling sounds die away.
She could have taken me at any time. She never did.
I was hers – she just needed to say it.

Alone.
The smell is heavenly – already the butter coats my tongue.
The pure ingredients, mine to devour.
A simple dish – mushroom, butter, garlic… and me.

STANLEY
by Misha Herwin

Mrs. Eleanor Mackenzie wrapped her sandwiches in greaseproof paper and packed them neatly into a Tupperware container. She placed the plastic box into her handbag along with some anti-bacterial wipes and a small thermos of tea. Then she put on her raincoat—because you can never be too sure of the weather, however bright the sun might be shining—made sure that the kitchen counters had been wiped down, the windows closed and the kettle unplugged, and let herself out of the house.

Halfway to the gate, she almost turned back. It was so long since she had been anywhere but the supermarket that her head felt as if it was suspended above her body and her feet had difficulty negotiating the pavement.

Don't be ridiculous, she told herself firmly. *Now that Henry has gone, you can do what you want, go where you want. Take a deep breath. Go to the top of the road. Turn left, not right, to the shops and walk down the hill.*

Following her own instructions, keeping her eyes firmly fixed on the horizon, blocking out the noise of the traffic, she made her way to the center of the town. Faced with crossing the dual carriageway, she stood hesitantly at the curb. The lights changed, and cars waited poised like athletes on the starting line. Mrs. Eleanor Mackenzie looked right then left, as she had been taught to do when she was a little girl.

"Come on, love. You don't want to stand around." An older woman wheeling a baby buggy came up beside her. "They'll be off again in a minute." She pushed the buggy onto the crossing, and emboldened by her action, Mrs. Eleanor Mackenzie followed.

The street on the other side was full of people. Mothers hurrying along small children, groups of girls giggling and gossiping. Friends talking, men trailing behind their wives. A lad with a dog on a leash. Another talking rapidly into his phone.

In the market square, a trader rapped out special offers. Punnets of pansies and primroses, trays of scarlet and pink fuchsias made splashes of color on the flower stall, the egg man chatted to a customer, a fat woman bargained over a packet of summer vests. Voices rose and fell; people lingered, and then moved on. Nothing remained still or silent.

Clutching the handle of her bag, Mrs. Eleanor Mackenzie hurried through the square and down into the underpass. There were some who found the tiled tunnel threatening, but for her it was a welcome respite, muffling the sound of the market and leading to a sunken garden. Circular in shape, its walls were covered in creepers, the beds in front of them filled with shrubs and flowers. In the middle of the garden, a bright display of red, yellow, orange, and purple primulas lapped around the paws of a wickerwork bear.

The animal had a smile on its face, or she imagined it must, as it stood there among the flowers watching the people who passed by or the one or two who chose to take time out of their busy lives to sit on a bench. It was something she had done as often as she could in the early days of Henry's illness, when it was still possible to leave him for an hour. As the years had gone by, she had thought longingly of stealing time to sit in this garden. Cradled below ground, sheltered from the weather yet open to the sun, it was warmer than the surrounding streets, making it a good place to sit even in winter and one where the homeless could find refuge.

They mostly kept to the fringes of the garden, men and women bundled up in blankets and sleeping bags, dreadlocked, greasy haired, and dirty. They would set up camp at the entrance to one of the tunnels, where, by averting her eyes, it was possible to ignore them.

Today, however, one of them had taken her bench. He sat comfortably on the seat she had promised herself, the one where she could sit and look at the bear. Dressed in what looked like army fatigues, he was older than the usual run of pale youths with chapped lips and pierced extremities. His dark hair, threaded with silver, was tied back in a ponytail with a leather thong. His skin was deeply tanned, his face lined, his eyes, when he looked at her, a vivid blue.

Mrs. Eleanor Mackenzie met his glance and looked hastily away. Clicking her tongue with disapproval, her eyes stung with disappointed tears as she settled herself on the next bench, far enough away not to be distressed by his smell, of tobacco and turpentine, yet close to the bear.

Balancing her handbag on her knees and keeping her heels together, she took out the flask and the plastic container. Placing them on the bench beside her, she wiped her hands on an antibacterial wipe before pouring herself a cup of tea. Sweet and warm, it slipped down easily.

The sun was warm on the back of her neck. The tea gave her strength, and she took out a sandwich. Egg and cress. Her favorite. Too pungent for some, but she relished the combination of fluffy egg and creamy mayo, offset by the fresh crunch of the cress.

Eyes half shut, she took a bite. It tasted as good as she remembered; poised for the next mouthful, however, she became aware of being watched. The homeless man on the next bench was looking at her. She turned her head sharply, preparing to glare, then was swept by a flush of guilt. Here she was, a woman, a widow, with her own house, a reasonable pension, sitting in the sun eating her lunch, while he, with nowhere to go and no one to care for him, was going hungry.

The half-eaten sandwich in her hand was an embarrassment. She had lost her appetite, but, with his eyes on her, she could hardly throw the unwanted food into a bin, from where—the thought was too horrible to contemplate—he might, if he were truly desperate, retrieve it. Nor could she put it back in the box, not now that she'd had it in her mouth.

"He's a goodun' that bear." His voice startled her. From her experience of destitute people on the streets, they rarely spoke beyond a muttered grunt for "any spare change Missus?" To be accosted in such a manner was so disconcerting that, instead of averting her eyes and ignoring the interruption, she responded.

"I've always liked him."

"It's the smile," the man said. "That's what does it."

"You see it too?" The sandwich slipped from her fingers and she left it lying on the bench as she turned to face him.

"Oh yes," he nodded. "But is it ironic or amused?"

"I've never thought about it." Mrs. Eleanor Mackenzie studied the wicker bear and wondered for a crazy moment what was going on in its head.

"If that's egg and cress, then I'll have it," the man said.

"No, no," her hand closed around the discarded sandwich. "I couldn't possibly. Here," she got up and carried the plastic box across to him. "Take this."

His fingers as he reached in to take the sandwich were rimed with dirt. The nails thick and black. Suppressing a shudder, Mrs. Eleanor Mackenzie took a step back. "Good sandwich. Real mayo?" the man said, and she noticed that he had swallowed before he'd spoken.

"Well, from a jar. I don't make my own." *Though I used to. Years ago when we had proper meals every evening and friends came round for supper at weekends.*

"Good enough, and on brown bread, too."

"The healthy alternative, and I prefer it to white."

"The unhealthy does you good too." He winked. Mrs. Eleanor Mackenzie took another step back. He held out the empty box. "Thanks for that. Greatly enjoyed it." She stared at the plastic container.

"I'm sorry. I haven't got any more." What should she do? Was he still hungry? Should she give him money? Everyone said you should not, that they would only spend it on drugs or alcohol, that the best way to help someone it his position was to give food or advice about how to seek help. But she did not know where someone in his position might go, or which agencies to contact.

The rectangular opaqueness of the box stretched between them. Contaminated by his filthy hands, how would she ever be able to use it again?

"You could always bring another couple of sarnies. Next time you're down here."

"I could." The relief was enormous. She would not have to dispose of the box, or use it herself, and it would still be fulfilling a useful purpose. "I will." She surprised herself by nodding briskly and smiling.

The following day, she prepared more egg and cress sandwiches and another flask of tea. The sun was still shining and the walk into town more pleasant than the day before. It was possible to look around her, to notice the vase of daffodils in a front window, a cat sunning itself on a wall, a girl, ears plugged with music, who nevertheless smiled as she passed.

He was there, on what she still considered her bench, and she handed over the food. He took one sandwich and, lifting it to his nose, breathed in the smell of egg.

"It's what you said you like." Why was she concerned about whether he liked the food she had brought? Surely having something to eat was enough.

"I did." He took a bite, then seeing her still standing schoolteacher-like above him, asked, "Aren't you having some?"

"I…" She had been so caught up in her preparations she had not thought of herself. "It's good to share." He held out the box. Mrs. Eleanor Mackenzie looked at the remaining sandwich. Prepared in near-sterile conditions, handled only by herself, wrapped in greaseproof paper straight from the roll, it was as germ free as it was possible to get, except that his fingers might have brushed it as he took his own out of the box; a flake of dirt, an invisible dusting of microbes, could have fallen onto the paper, worked its way through the protective covering, and even now be burrowing its way into the bread.

"But you're hungry," she stammered. He smiled.

"As much for company as anything."

Mrs. Eleanor Mackenzie took a deep breath. Years of unremitting war on germs had not kept the cancer that devoured Henry at bay. She took the remaining sandwich. The man patted the bench, and she sat down. Not too close beside him. There were bugs that could leap from one body to another, and the heavy oily smell that clung to him disturbed her senses. She tasted it on her sandwich, and it snagged at elusive memories that she could not fully recall.

They did not speak, and when they had finished, she took the box, packed it away, nodded her head, and left.

Walking to the bus stop, a sulphurous taste rose to her mouth, and before she could stop herself, a bubble of gas escaped her lips. Perhaps it was time to move on from egg and cress. As the bus lumbered up the hill, she considered various combinations, from cheese and pickle to smoked salmon and shrimp.

Somewhat extravagant. Henry's voice in her head made her start. Her husband of forty years sounded mean and petty. Had he always been like that? Mrs. Eleanor McKenzie tightened her hold on the handle of her bag.

Of course her sandwich-eating companion should not have lost his job and his home. It was up to everyone to take responsibility for their own lives, to make provision for the bad times as well as the good. Just as Henry had always done. Only a few days ago she would have shared her husband's view, but as the bus lurched to a stop and she made her way to the door, she found herself shaking her head.

Life was unpredictable. Not all the insurance policies or pension plans that Henry had so carefully organized had been able to halt the relentless progress of his cancer. Bad luck, bad management, a single mistake could happen to anyone. Who was she, who had led such a safe and protected life, to judge?

"Smoked salmon and cream cheese bagels. With a flask of freshly brewed coffee," she told the empty house. "I think," she added a little more hesitantly, "that he'll like those, and I know I will."

Her confidence lasted until she was making her way down into town. When she entered the garden, however, she hesitated. What if she had made a mistake? If she was being taken advantage of? If he was priming her for more than a few sandwiches, that he was planning to rob her, or break into her house, or con her of her life savings?

Never trust a stranger had been one of Henry's maxims. Better keep yourself to yourself rather than risk disappointment, had been the way she had lived for the whole of her life.

She cast a quick glance at the bench. Empty, he was not there. Relief ballooned through her, followed by a strange, sinking feeling.

And then, there he was, coming through the tunnel that led to the supermarket carpark. His eyes crinkled with pleasure when he saw her, and she was starting forward, all her fears forgotten.

"I brought salmon today. I think we've had enough egg," she said.

"Egg makes wind." He grinned. "At least it does for me. I'm Stanley." He held out his hand. She took it.

"I am Eleanor." She was going to add Mackenzie, but there was something about the firmness and warmth of his grip that distracted her.

Smoked salmon and cream cheese, shrimp and mayo, chicken and grapes, the best ham and organic tomatoes. On white bread, on wholemeal, on stoneground, focaccia, bruschetta. Her repertoire grew.

They met at least twice a week throughout the spring and summer. On Tuesdays and Thursdays, she would go into town and they would sit in comfortable silence, side by side. Occasionally, she commented on the weather, or the flower display chosen by the council for this season, and he would respond by describing the expression on the face of the wicker bear in reaction to the garish colors of the planting.

The days grew cooler. She invested in a thermal bag, looked up recipes for hot fillings and spicy stews.

What would he do when the weather changed? Where would he

go? She put clean sheets on the bed in the spare room.

On a chilly October day when the sun was struggling through the morning mirk, she packed two cartons of boeuf bourguignon into her bag. In the market she chatted with the egg man, and smiled at the lady on the bric-a-brac stall, before buying a loaf of freshly baked bread from the deli and going down through the tunnel and out into the hazy mist of the underground garden. The ground had been cleared, ready for the winter, and the bear stood forlornly among the empty flower beds, but as she approached their bench, the sun finally broke free of the cloud bathing the garden with golden light.

As if in a film where time slips between past and present, she saw him sitting there. He looked younger, his shoulders straighter, hair darker, face less lined as he turned to greet her.

"Stanley." She blinked to clear her vision.

"I'm Eric, his son."

Anger swirled through her. "You mean he has a family? A family that lets him live on the streets?"

"My father wasn't homeless."

"Wasn't? I don't understand."

Eric smiled wryly. "Dad was always a free spirit. He lived and..." He paused. "He died as he wanted."

The garden spun; the breath was sucked from her lungs. The bags dropped to the ground, and she was aware, somewhere in the back of her head, of a voice telling her about a heart attack and something he had to show her.

"If you are up to it, I can take you there now." Eric's words finally made sense.

"But I was going to..." She had imagined him in her house, sharing sandwiches and coffee at lunch time, a stew for their dinner, and bacon and eggs in the morning. Or would it be toast and that burnt orange marmalade the color of sun through stained glass?

While she had been spinning these dreams, what had he been doing?

Eric took her arm and led her through the shadow of the underpass that led out into the supermarket carpark. He drove them to an older part of town, where large Victorian houses bordered long-established allotments.

"Dad broke all the rules," Eric said, and he unlocked the gate and led her up a narrow path to a wooden cabin. "You're not supposed to live here, but there was no telling him." He pushed open the door, and she was assailed by the familiar scent of oil and turpentine.

Every surface was hung with paintings, more were stacked against the walls, and there were charcoal sketches on the worktable, all of the same subject.

"He was painting me?" Eleanor walked across to the easel and looked at the painting. The picture showed a woman on a bench, her face illuminated by sunlight, every crease and wrinkle carefully delineated but painted with such love, a love that was reflected in the eyes of the sitter and the smile of the wickerwork bear.

SABLÉS, THE SANDY COOKIES
by Lynn Hoffman

old cook says he likes the grit
in things and thoughts and wine and songs
he wants, he says, some scratch with his sweet
some poke with his joke and smoke.

Beat butter and sugar. Add egg, vanilla and blend.

butterbaker says she understands and if
she wasted oven space on
what weren't there, she'd
run off a batch of wish-that-it-scratched

Add flour to butter mixture.

the soup's away, the sauce is shiny, chilled
he'd love to stay so he has to go
her back is turned, his apron's off
her fingers stiff, his face gone soft

Do not overmix the dough.

wait, she says. take these with you
sablés she says, no one makes them anymore
all sandy beach and not much ocean
the butter-cow comes at the very end.

Bake until golden brown around the edges.

young cooks laughing, shouting
counting time, slapping pans and playing games
old cook and butterbaker standing close
still at work and moving home.

BOUILLABAISSE
by John C. Mannone

Naked, she stirs herbs and spices into the porcelain pot simmering the seafood broth. He sits on a bungalow barstool, legs crossed, a shower towel draped over his lap, admiring her creativity. She winks back. They are both ravenous, with an appetite for more.

The stock, infused with shrimp shells and bony salmon parts, is tempered with bay leaf, orange peel, peppercorn, and thyme, soon ready for the collage of marine delicacies. Before making love, they worked their fingers, raking the ocean sand for clams, scooping them into the basket. He scrubs the tan and mahogany brown shells clean, lightly steams them open for their juice to be added to the soup, while the lobster watches him pull byssal hairs from the blue ribbed mussels.

Soon, steam will waft them open, too. In the shower, thick heat condenses on semi-opaque glass. Eyes intoxicated. Her flesh, sumptuous, his, firm. Both wrap around each other in shower mist. In the hot froth, mackerel, grouper, and scrod swim with just a few plum tomatoes for texture and color, drunk in a sea of Pouilly-Fuissé, a pale and delicate Chardonnay, for the marriage with the lobster still slippered in its shell; so too the shrimp and spider crab, the octopus and scallop. The union is always an ecstasy.

He slips over to her. The stove is hot. They are careful not to touch. They tremor in the heat—the celery, leeks, and Yukon gold. She closes her eyes for a moment, smells the salt and seething sea spray from below. He kisses her softly, picks up the towel that slid off his lap unto the floor. She opens her eyes that glisten like olive oil on shimmering liquid. Her tongue licks the essence of soup from a long-handled spoon. She smiles with approval, and he is anxious for some.

The toaster-oven bell signals the crusty French bread is ready to be lavished with red-peppered rouille. She ladles the spicy mixture deep into broad blue bowls. Threads of saffron float on the surface—burnt orange and fire red stigmas of lilac-colored crocus flowers—necessary for the magic of the meal, for the satisfying. It always is.

STOLEN LOVE
by Miguel A. Rueda

Luciana "Lulu" Migliaccio's home resembled the aftermath of a small Midwestern town following a level-five tornado crammed into a twenty by twenty studio apartment. But the objects on the table near the door were arranged in precise, matrix-like order.

Stale cookies—sugar and with various fillings—lined the front edge; dehydrated donuts—previously jelly or crème filled—occupied the next row; and several small display signs—one declaring a "2-for-1" sale, another a "Baker's Dozen" special—were against the wall. The arrangement created a tiered effect around the table's focal point, a framed newspaper clipping.

Picking up the picture, she gazed at the man standing in front of DaVinci's Italian Bakery. The article's headline read, "Enzo DaVinci Carries on Family Tradition in Brother's Memory." She held the thin wooden frame with her fingertips so as not to dislodge any of the paint pulled from the wall when she had stolen it. The memento, along with everything else on the table, had been taken from DaVinci's.

The smell of anise floated into her apartment. "Enzo must be making biscotti," she muttered.

When baked, the extract produced a distinct aroma that comforted her. She loved to dunk the oblong biscuit in coffee and let the hard shell soften. She closed her eyes and imagined the texture of the dough melting against her tongue, the feel of the softened hazelnuts filling her mouth. She smiled at the thought. It was heaven.

She opened her eyes, kissed the glass, and placed the frame back on the table. She put on her bright-red overcoat and left her apartment, which was one floor above the kitchen of DaVinci's bakery.

Enzo was indeed making biscotti. He had just pulled out the long, flat loaves to let them cool before slicing them into their familiar shapes and returning them to the oven. This process gave the twice-baked cookie its literal name.

DaVinci's front half had tables and display cases with a one-way mirror separating it from the kitchen so that Enzo could see what was going on while he worked. The entire store took up a third of a block, with the entrance to the apartments above the stores at the opposite end.

He inhaled deeply and let his mind return to the small town near Sicily where he grew up. His grandmother had lived in the tiny kitchen of the apartment on the second floor of his parents' home. She gifted him his love of baking, especially bread and desserts. Food made her happy, which made him happy. In his mind, the scent was the smell of home—of love—of eternity.

"Uncle Enzo." The squeak and subsequent thud of the door separating the kitchen and retail spaces broke Enzo's daydream. "She's back."

Even though he had lived in the United States for the last decade, Enzo spoke with a thick Italian accent. It added a poetic lilt to everything he said. "Who is back, Gio?"

"That woman who keeps shoplifting. The fat lady...."

"*Basta, Giovanni!* Do not disrespect anyone. Your Nonna looks the same way, no?"

Gio nodded, "Yes uncle, you're right."

Enzo peered into the shop. She stood by the door like a mouse poking her head through a hole checking for a cat, ready to flee at the first sign of danger.

Enzo said, "That woman is the perfect woman, Gio. She is, eh, Rubenesque."

Gio's face skewed. "Ruben-who?"

"Rubenesque. Like the woman's body painted by Rubens? You are not taught this in your fancy college?"

"Do you mean Rubik's, like a Rubik's cube?"

Enzo glared at Gio. "Si, nephew. I mean she is a Rubik's Cube." Shaking his head he looked back at her, "She is not a square. What person is square?"

Gio mumbled, "Well, you're a bit of a square."

Enzo threw a handful of flour at Gio. "Kids today, no respect. What with your, eh, Facepage and constant tweetering." He pointed to Gio, "Go out there. Apologize to that pretty lady."

"Um, no. I'm not doing that. What would I even say? I'm sorry I think you need to lose a few pounds, but my uncle thinks you're cute?"

Enzo blushed, "No, no, no, do not mention me!" He thought for a moment. "Ah, tell her she won something. A, eh, free coffee for being our hundredth customer today. Go. And ask her name."

Gio smirked, "You want me to ask her name? Why would I...?" Realization came to him. "Oh, you do like her. That's why you let her get away with taking stuff."

"Gio, stop. That is absurd."

"Oh really, Unc? I've known you ever since my pop got sick and you came to help us keep the bakery. You weren't married in Italy, and you've never dated here. You're always in here, baking. You took care of us when my dad passed away, but we're good now. I've seen the way you look at her. Go ask her out."

Enzo looked at Gio, and then back out the window, "Okay, Nephew, I will do that." He wiped his hands on his apron, then ran his fingers through his hair, adding in more flour than he wiped away. He took a deep breath and walked out.

When he opened the door, Lulu was trying to slide a plate of cellophane-wrapped cookies under her coat. The hinges' squeal drew Lulu's attention. When she saw Enzo looking at her, she dropped the cookies and ran out.

"Wait!" Enzo rushed after her.

He picked up the plate and followed her. He saw a flash of red as she ducked into the entrance for the apartments. Hurrying through after her, he found a second, locked door leading into the building.

He looked around and saw an intercom unit. A quarter-sized glass bubble sat atop a mesh grill covering the speaker. Four handwritten name tags sat beneath it: Sam Cohen, another with indecipherable Chinese lettering, a third that had several small bats and a skull sketched onto it, and finally, in perfect script, the name Lulu Migliaccio.

Guessing that it had to be her, he pushed, and believing it was necessary, held the button next to her name. The electronic ringing from the speaker stopped when a small lightbulb inside the button lit up.

He heard a woman's voice, out of breath, quiet and sounding far away. "Hello, can I help you?"

"*Ciao*. Eh, hello *Signorina Migliaccio*. This is Enzo DaVinci from the bakery. You dropped your *struffoli*." He released the button.

She had heard him speak in the bakery, but he'd never said her name. When he pronounced Migliaccio with a proper Italian accent, it sounded operatic. She stared at Enzo on the small monitor set into the wall above her shrine to him. His voice, deep and exotic, wrapped her in a warm blanket of love. Her mind drifted on the possibilities.

Enzo placed the cookies on the package shelf below the mailboxes and pushed the button. "Hello. Eh, Miss Lulu, are you still there?"

His voice pulled her back to the present.

"Yes, I'm here."

"Your cookies are left by the door. Eh, if you are free, I would like you to join me at eight o'clock tonight for coffee and dessert." He released the button. Then quickly, and unnecessarily, he pushed it again, "My, eh, treat."

He stepped back and waited for her response.

Lulu watched him fidget. In the mirrored wall of the lobby, he noticed his hair was speckled with clumps of dough and streaks of flour. He licked his fingers and tried to brush it away, succeeding only in making it stick out at odd angles in some places and plastering against his scalp in others. She laughed at the short, chubby man on the screen who had no idea she could see him.

"Enzo, yes. I would be happy to."

She saw him smile and reach for the button. He paused and, unaware she could hear, whispered, "Vincenzo DaVinci, you are going to marry this woman."

He pushed the button, "Thank you. I will see you tonight."

In the weeks before that evening, Enzo had watched her from behind his mirrored partition. Every morning as she walked past the store to the bus stop on the corner, she glanced in. If it were empty, she would open the door and grab anything close enough to steal without having to enter. Enzo began to leave items near the entrance, each day moving them a little farther inside. One day, she had made it halfway to the counter when someone walked in behind her. Startled, she turned and scurried out, only stopping long enough to grab a framed newspaper article off the wall.

Since that day, he had vowed to confront her. Not about the thefts, but about his feelings for her. Despite her size, he knew she was invisible to all those around her but him; he saw her as demure and fragile. They had to be alike: lonely, but too shy to do anything about it.

Enzo closed early that evening, returned home, and showered, making sure that his hair was combed neatly and remiss of extraneous baking supplies. At eight o'clock, he walked to her apartment and pressed the intercom. It rang only once. "Hello, Enzo. I'll be right down."

"*Sì*, I will wait." He released the button and waited a full fifteen minutes before reaching to press it again.

A familiar fragrance stopped him. He caught a whiff of *Biagiotti Roma*, the same perfume his grandmother wore. Lulu opened the door. The voluptuous beauty he had been searching for all of his adult life stood before him. Her eyes sparkled in the dim light. His voice barely audible, he said, *"Buona sera."* He coughed to regain the power of speech. "Eh, good evening, Lulu." He held out his arm for her to hold as they walked back to the bakery.

He had set a table up in the center of his kitchen; he always felt most secure surrounded by the equipment and tools he loved. They talked, nervously at first since they knew virtually nothing about each other. Neither could admit they had been secretly stalking the other.

He had made mini-cannolis overflowing with a vanilla-bean-infused ricotta filling. By the end of the evening, they had made plans to meet the next night.

Enzo walked her home and returned to his kitchen. He wasn't surprised when he found that one of the espresso demitasses was missing. He looked up toward the apartment above him and blew a kiss.

"One day, all of this will belong to you. No matter if you take it piece by piece or all at once."

They continued to meet every night at the same time. Enzo would make special versions of the desserts that made the bakery popular. *Cannoncini* filled with dark-chocolate mousse, linzer cookies with raspberry jam that had a perfect balance of sweet and tart, each tiny seed exploded with flavor. Enzo always served them in odd numbers so that Lulu could have the last one.

At end of their first week, Lulu stopped stealing from the bakery. That evening, she had snuck out with a half-filled silver creamer in her purse. She had been nervous, and secretly excited, as he walked her home. Inside her apartment, she looked at the table she had piled with everything she had pilfered and realized that she no longer needed that thrill to feel connected to him. She now had all of him.

She threw away everything with the exception of the framed newspaper. She had other plans for that.

On their one-month anniversary, Enzo set the table with a pure-white tablecloth, linen napkins, and two slender ivory candles in silver candlesticks. He replaced the usual porcelain plates with fine Italian china that he had shipped from his hometown. In the center of the table sat a plate of seven *pignoli* cookies. He had baked the patterns of the small pine nuts into the cookies in pairs: two stars, two squares, and two circles. The seventh unique shape lay hidden beneath the others.

Lulu arrived, carrying a flat, rectangular box.

When she saw the special setting, she said, "Enzo, this is beautiful, I mean, *bellissimo*." She had been studying Italian using a book that she had actually paid for. "Is this a special occasion?"

"*Sì* Lulu, it is." He pointed to the package. "You have something special for me?"

"Oh, this? Yes. Perhaps we should sit."

Enzo held the chair for her—just as he did every night—then sat and poured them both coffee.

"Enzo, before you open this, there is something you need to know." She handed him the box. "I have a problem that I'm working on. I steal things. Little things, nothing big or expensive."

Enzo chuckled. "*Mio amore*, eh, my love, I know. I have always known."

He opened the box. He saw the picture she had taken from his wall.

She had reframed the clipping in an ornate gold frame she had purchased from an antique store.

"This is beautiful. *Grazia*."

"But Enzo, I.... "

"No." Enzo reached across the table and placed his finger on her lips. "No more talk of the past. Tonight is about the future."

She was too embarrassed to make eye contact with the man to whom she had just confessed her darkest secret, a secret he had accepted without question. Tears welled in her eyes. She tasted a cookie. The inner dough was soft and moist, the pignoli supple on her tongue. They reached the seventh, hidden cookie. Slightly larger than the others, the toasted nuts were set in the shape of a heart.

Enzo smiled and played the game he did every night. "I am full, Lulu. You take the last."

She looked at the remaining cookie, the candlelight flickering off the glaze baked onto its surface. She knew that each pine nut had been touched by Enzo's loving hands. She began to cry.

Enzo's smile fell; he started to stand. *"Mio amore,* what is wrong?"

Lulu stopped him. "Sit, I'm okay. It's just so beautiful, everything. You're just so lovely to me."

She picked up the cookie and bit it in half.

She chewed once. Stopped. Looked at Enzo.

He rose and stepped around the table, kneeled, and took her hand.

"Signorina Luciana Migliaccio. Mi vuoi sposare? Lulu, my love, marry me?"

The musical poetry of his words, spoken with his beautiful accent, overwhelmed her. She began to shake. Between the excitement and emotion of the moment, she started coughing. Then she swallowed.

Enzo jumped up. "Lulu, did you...?"

Lulu grabbed her throat. She looked as though she wanted to somehow find a way to jump back in time.

He took her hand. "Don't worry, we will get help." He led her to the door, stopping before opening it. "Lulu, I have to know." He looked into her eyes, "Will you?"

No longer concerned about her predicament, she calmed. *"Sì, Vincenzo DaVinci. Ti amo."*

TROLLING THE UNKNOWN
by Dianna Henning

In the other room is a sky where you eat at the table of stars.
A handsome God trolling the universe drops by and sits beside you.
He is not well-versed in poetry but knows volumes about myth.

Eyeing your plate's abundance, some of your spaghetti moves
to Alaska, and the puzzled God asks, *Where the hell is Alaska?*
With little hope of illuminating him on earth's geography,

you stick to your solar system and say, *Far off as Neptune, of course.*
He speaks fondly of Neptune's rapturous winds
and inquires; *Want to troll the unknown with me?*

Your response, perhaps curt, implies you
already troll the unknown using tiny nymphs as bait,
your spaghetti reminding you it's no worm.

Such a wise guy this God who lectures, *Line control is a problem
with nymphs.* Fed up, and somewhat well fed,
escape becomes your only option. You've been outwitted,

and you determine that the next time you dine
with a God you'd best brush up on your angler techniques.

SEEING THE FORK FIRST TIME
by Betsy Fogelman Tighe

In my hand it looks like a wand, tapping the head of a rabbit sporting
a pink ribbon. It dips under the food, the lift piled with cracked bricks.
The scratching of the fork on plate is a primitive tune
I've heard daily but not noted. A shovel in dirt. The fork trembles
a bit, tentative to approach the food, yet firm, like the first kiss,
sure of what it wants but uncertain of what it will get. The fork
takes my heat, like sheets, or the body of a man lying next to me.
Unmalleable since inception, solid and useful. If people were more
like things they'd cause less suffering. The fork dips, the swan
leaning its breast into the water. It lifts a bit of bok choy and rice,
suspended in air, the load coming off the docked freighter. The space
between the tines is sexual, like the center of a woman's body,
the gap between her thighs as she walks. The fork rests
by the plate, askew, a little dirty.

DIVING GIRL'S DINING GUIDE
by Peter Marcus

Tako, pulipo, ocapodi, sannakji, polvo, pulpo, ahtapot.
Char-grilled, wood-roasted, bedded on arugula, soaked gooey-raw
in wasabi, sashimi-style divided by thin slices of lemon, rubbed
in basil, oregano, fennel, dotted with capers and olive tapenade,
sprinkled with chili flakes, garnished with a yellow tomato salsa.
Even without the English translation, you insist, "Let's order
the octopus!" Fine dear, but please consider the more informed
I've become about their oceanic lives, the more reluctant my desire
to indulge. Their capacity for long-term memory, how their pliant
flesh senses light. Did you know that octopi engage in play?
That they mate only once per life—beacons of devotion and fidelity.
You swiftly dismiss my misgivings with Buddha-like detachment.
Even after I inform you of their ability to fast for six months—
outdoing Thich Nhat Hanh and the Dalai Lama. After downing two
stiff cocktails, I inevitably acquiesce to your request. "You're right.
There's nothing more enticing on the menu." After we order, you
raise your glass of Riesling to each added fact: both sexes have three
hearts and each male sports a detachable penis that rapidly grows
back. I succumb because I want you really sensuous tonight, like
that lustful lady in the Hokusai print, "Diving Girl with Octopus."
I want you ravenous and rapturous as we sink into our memory-
foam. My other solace as we divide the charred tentacles: at least
its sagacious eyes are not staring up at us from the black cast iron.

FRENCH COOKING
by Mary B. Moore

The chocolate in the beef bourguignon is meant
to offset the tannin in all that red wine
I used to drink which pinks my cells still
the sauce will be piquant like the scent
of you after sex or the bouquet
of roses you bring me with the wide-eyed
look of one without fore-sorrows

The worry god who rode my left hand
turn signal—*click, click, tsk, tsk*—his Om
a battery of consonants, luckily can't
abide French cooking, so thumbs
a ride on somebody else's rearview hindsight. Thyme
beef, shallots, wine, the sauce intensifies
as it simmers. We're steeped in each other. Our scents rhyme.

OFF THE MENU
by Paulene Turner

Dinan, France, 1944

He's back again. At table eight.

Earlier than usual, the morning sun turns his hair a rusty gold, like the toffee crust on a crème brûlée. As he smiles, a dimple appears in his right cheek. I feel my taut lips relax and hope I'm not smiling back. It wouldn't look good.

Rainer is a German soldier in the force occupying my home town of Dinan, northern France.

"Bonjour Simone," he says in heavily accented French.

"What do you want Herr?" I'm snappish as usual.

"A word?"

We are in Le Paturage du Ciel (Heaven's Pasture), a bistro where I work just outside town. Jean-Claude, the owner and chef, runs it from his home—four tables in the front room, six more in the gravel garden with upturned crates as furniture. Behind the house is a pasture where he grows vegetables and herbs for our specialty: crepes.

Until recently, all our customers were French. Then some German soldiers found us and spread the word. Now, at lunchtime, the place swarms with them, like an infestation of cockroaches we can't stomp on or shoo away.

The first time he came to the bistro, Rainer sat at table eight, a sunny spot in the middle of the garden.

"What do you want, Herr?" I said, my standard opening to our German customers, cold as a Russian winter.

He turned to me, blue eyes curious, mouth ready to smile. "I'd like to know your name."

"Are you ordering me to tell you?"

"I give no orders here, I only make requests."

"Well I have a request," I said. "That you place your food order or leave so someone else may take your place."

His expression deflated like a soufflé inspected too soon. I left him studying the menu while I served another table—some French neighbors. As we exchanged news about people we knew who'd been hurt or killed "by the Germans" (I said loudly), I felt his attention on us. A sneaky glance revealed a muscle clenching on his jaw. Good, let it stay clenched.

I took my time with the French people, and then went back.

"Okay, what's good here?" he said, still pleasant, though I could see it took more effort.

"If you're asking about the food, it all is. If you mean the people, I'd say everyone not wearing a uniform is good."

I thought he might lose it at that point. Part of me wanted him to. I was just so angry about the Germans in our town, about everything to do with the war. It felt as if not blood, but hot fury and hate flowed through my veins.

Jean-Claude and I looked on it as a patriotic duty to be as rude as possible to the Germans who came here, just short of being shot. Things were touch and go sometimes.

Like now, with Rainer. I watched his chest slowly expand within his green-gray German coat, and then deflate as he exhaled. After that, he placed his order, chewed silently through his food, and left.

I was surprised to see him back the next day.

"My name is Rainer," he began. "And you are...?"

"Simone."

He smiled as if it was some kind of victory, which made me regret answering.

"I've always wanted to come to France," he said. "Now I'm here, it's everything I imagined it would be."

"Join the army," I said. "See the world, meet people from other countries, then shoot them."

His mouth went slack. I think he was genuinely hurt. "I wish the circumstances were different," he stammered, "...but are all French women as...forthright as you?"

"What do you expect, Herr? You are not on holiday here. Tell me, in Germany, do you barge into your neighbors' homes without invitation, leave your muddy boot prints on their floors, and then expect cake?"

"No, of course not. I...I'm sorry."

I should have felt triumphant—I had struck a blow for national pride. But somehow I didn't.

"There was an especially annoying German in here today," I said, as Jean-Claude and I washed up that afternoon. "I hope he doesn't come in again."

"It's good not to let the Germans get too comfortable," said Jean Claude. "But be careful you don't go too far, Simone. These men are not clowns. They are killers. Never forget that."

He was back the next day, like a cold you couldn't shake off.

"Can I have a plate of frogs' legs?" he asked.

"Sorry, frogs' legs are off the menu."

Most Germans wanted to try frogs' legs. Denying them the chance—though we had a plentiful supply—was our form of French resistance. That, and spitting on their food.

"No frogs' legs?" said Rainer. "Okay, then I'll have the…" He broke off to watch Jean-Claude carry a plate of fried legs to the French people at the next table. He raised his eyebrows at me. I raised my chin. "…I'll have the spring crepe," he said. "If you still have any of those?"

A couple of days later, we got some tragic news. Daniel, our goat cheese supplier, had been shot in town. He was a big, hairy guy with a quick smile. I'd known him since I was a girl. He was also an active member of the French resistance. His loss hit me, hit us all, hard.

As soon as Rainer came in, I think he could tell something was wrong. He sat in his usual place, but didn't get comfortable. One look at my face and he stood straight back up again. "Perhaps I should eat elsewhere today?"

"Yes, why don't you," I said. "You could try Munchen, or Hannover, or some other place in Germany!"

Head bowed, he crunched his way across the gravel towards the street.

"Herr, wait!" I called. He turned back. "You might as well stay. The money you spend, we'll give to Daniel's widow to help pay for his burial."

He sat down. "I am very sorry," he said, removing his hat.

Bitter words swam on my tongue. What right did he have to be sorry, when Daniel's murderer was one of his own countrymen? Who knew? Maybe it was even Rainer himself who had pulled the trigger? But I held them back.

"Thank you," I murmured instead.

We were extra busy that day. The lunch tables turned over three times. Towards the end of our service, three Germans sat at one of the indoor tables. They spat as they spoke and filled the room with their braying laughs and ugly consonants.

The worst of the three was a tall man with a long face like a horse and cruel eyes. They wanted frogs' legs.

"Frogs' legs are off the menu," I said, no hint of apology.

"But I just saw you take a plate to that French woman there."

"They were our last legs."

"I don't believe you, Fraulein," said the man.

"Pfff, I don't care what you believe, Monsieur."

The sizzling in the kitchen seemed loud as all went quiet around us. Then it stopped altogether, as Jean-Claude's bulky frame filled the kitchen doorway, his face pouchy with worry.

"This is the third time I have been here and you have given me this lie," said the soldier. "It is an insult to me. It is an insult to Germany."

"You are an insult to me and France," I said. "Get out of the restaurant. And don't come back again or next time I'll put poison in your food!"

Horseface drew his gun. The shiny barrel of the weapon was a long, dark tunnel of death thrust in my face. But I stuck my chin out at him—unwilling, unable to back down.

And then the back of a gray-green uniform blocked my view of the man, as Rainer stood between me and his fellow soldier, hands up in a gesture of surrender.

"The lady is not lying," he said. (One of my French patrons translated the German conversation for me later.) "I've eaten frogs' legs in this restaurant before. They're not as flavorsome as I'd hoped. They taste like fish."

Jean-Claude came out. "Monsieur, regrettably frogs' legs are in erratic supply these days. If you wish to try a plate, perhaps we can place a special order for you and your friends for the next time you grace us with your presence."

A deadly silence followed. And then the double click of a gun, primed to shoot. But Rainer stayed put.

"The crepes here are very good," he said. "Much better than fishy frogs' legs."

The man put his gun away but continued to shoot death stares at me. I shot mine right back.

"Why don't you do the cooking for a while, Simone?" said Jean-Claude. "I will serve the customers."

Later, as I saw Rainer about to leave, I called out. "Monsieur, wait!"

I threw off my apron and rushed out to the garden. "I did not ask for your help," I said. "I do not need help from a German."

It took him a moment to process my words, the smile lines rearranging themselves into confusion.

"I apologize, Simone," he said. "For my actions and those of my fellow soldiers."

"And for your information," I said, "frogs' legs do not taste like fish. They're more like chicken. Everyone knows that."

Jean-Claude and I were a little worried for the next few days that Horseface and his friends might try some violent retribution. But we didn't see them again. Presumably, they'd moved on to bully some other poor French restauranteur.

On his next visit, I didn't spit in Rainer's food. And, as he gave his crepe order, I said: "If you'd like the frogs' legs, we have some today."

He smiled so warmly in response I almost cancelled the order.

There were a few days when he didn't come in, and I found I was anxious and unsettled. Whether I was worried something bad had happened to him or he was doing something bad to someone else, I couldn't say.

Whenever he turned up after an absence, I gave him an extra serving of French pride. "Thank you, I enjoyed that," he said, after finishing his meal.

"You did? What a pity!"

Over the next two weeks, he sought opportunities to tell me about himself or ask about me. He was a bookkeeper who liked art, especially impressionistic style paintings—"though my family says it is not true art." He loved the spontaneity of France—"so different from Germany. Not as efficient, but exhilarating."

He got a few things out of me too, like how I'd lost my mother when I was four and dreamt of one day having my own bistro by the water.

"The war won't last forever," he said. "You will have your restaurant, Simone, I feel sure of it."

"But what will be left then?" I said. "Will the whole world be German? Will I have to put Bratwurst and sauerkraut on the menu?"

"I certainly hope not," he said.

We both grinned at that.

Now, he's here again, and it scares me how glad I am about that.

"Simone, come for a walk with me?" he says.

"No!" I hiss.

"I need to talk to you."

I send him off to wait for me at the oak tree at the bottom of the pasture, where we won't be seen. Ten minutes later, I hurry down the road to join him. The air is scented with warm earth and herbs. The field is a vibrant green, and tall stalks sway in the breeze, like spies trying to catch glimpse.

"I can't believe you would ask me for a walk," I say, storming over. "What would people think if they saw me strolling with a German, who, for all I know, might have killed their brothers or sons?"

"It's not personal. I fight to defend the people around me. No more, no less."

"That is just words, blah-blah-blah that tell me nothing."

"We are both creatures of our time, Simone," he said. "Floating with the current, no real control over where we go."

"You say that, but you can control how far you go in fulfilling your duties to your country. You are responsible for that. And for how much you enjoy it."

"You're right," he says, sighing audibly. "We will all have to account for our actions one day."

His blue eyes have a faraway quality, as if he's in a dark tunnel looking towards the light.

I wonder what he wants from me. Romance? Am I another French delicacy to try before going home? That's not going to happen. Though standing here, I feel intensely vulnerable as I realize just how much I like him. His patience, his strength, his humility.

"I must say goodbye," he says. "I'll be leaving soon."

"I hope you don't expect me to kiss you?"

"No! I mean…I can't say I haven't imagined what it might be like. But I wouldn't ask it of you."

"Good, because I would rather cut off my lips than kiss an enemy soldier."

He smiles and shakes his head. "Simone, so much fire in you. It is admirable, but very dangerous. Please, I urge you, have the feeling—but don't show so much."

"I will show as much as I wish. You Germans deserve it, and I am not afraid."

"You should be afraid," he said. "I have seen people killed, and brutally, with far less provocation. I do not want you to be among them."

I wasn't sure what to say to that.

"Why did you ask me to come here?"

He tells me he overheard Horseface and his friends talking about getting revenge for the frogs' legs incident before they leave Dinan.

"You should tell Jean-Claude to close the restaurant for a while, and stay away from the house. I don't want anything bad to happen to either of you."

As furious as I am at this news—and I am, ranting and raging so fast Rainer can't keep up—I cannot be angry with him. I know he's taken a risk coming to warn us. I'm grateful for that.

"You know, you're not what I expected a German soldier to be," I say.

"You are everything and more than I hoped for in a French woman."

Five Years Later

I've just finished setting for dinner in my restaurant, Neptune's Pasture, on the water, in Dinan. It's a warm evening. The breeze carries a scent of the sea and freshly turned fields. I take a minute to pull apart a baguette left from the morning to throw to the ducks on the water.

As I turn back, I see a customer at an outdoor table—a man in a dark suit.

"Are you ready to order, sir?"

"Yes I am," he says. He has a heavy German accent, which still makes me bristle. I try to glimpse his face, but it's hidden behind the menu.

"May I have the frogs' legs please?"

"I'm sorry, Herr, but frogs' legs are off."

Rainer lowers the menu, a broad smile on his tanned face. "Now, why doesn't that surprise me?"

MAN AND SUPERWOMAN
by Eric Paul Shaffer

We met when she caught my flaming plane falling from the sky.
She ripped through the fuselage and pulled me from the controls,
and we surprised each other with our sudden attraction. There,

among the clouds, as broken wings and wheels hurtled to earth,
        we shyly introduced ourselves. In mid-air, I asked her out.
She accepted. We flew to a café, shared fresh-ground Colombian

beans in a French press and a slice of blueberry cheesecake,
        exchanged numbers, and the rest is mystery and delight.
She is gentle, but with super powers, sometimes, things little

and large do get broken. Once, she tore the shower curtain
from the rod, and the rod from the wall, with an inattentive flick
of the wrist, but then, she emerged from the bathroom wrapped

in a pale green robe, smelling of strawberries, cradled a phonebook
        in her arm, and raised a flashlight above her head, giggling
till I saw the resemblance with Lady Liberty beyond her in the bay,

framed in the view. When we married, we exchanged gold bands,
but she wears no ring now since so many have been burned away,
        blown off, or broken in the chaotic course of fighting crime,

and she hangs the newest band on a titanium chain hidden beneath
her impervious blue suit. We both agree knowing the ring is there
is good enough, gold and warm against her invincible flesh. Now,

as man and superwoman, her secret identity is no secret to me.
I know all the retirement plans, the ATM codes, and the names
and numbers on every insurance policy, and, yes, we celebrate

our anniversaries and holidays like everyone else. Every year,
we fix our Thanksgiving dinner together. She thaws the bird
in seconds with the heat of her gaze, and among pots of yams

THE WAY TO MY HEART

        and carrots, she places the pan one-handed in the oven.
For the sake of tradition, and the gradual scent, we cook the turkey
for the proper hours as so many others do. She mashes potatoes,

prepares the peas, gravy, and rolls, sets the table in seconds,
        and then relaxes on the couch, watching the parade on TV
while I spend an hour making my famous stuffing. I use cubed

sourdough, butter, sage, and thyme. Later, her cousin arrives
from the sky, with nowhere else to go, orphaned, too, of parents
and planet, and a little blue about his missing worlds. We cheer

him up and cater to his every holiday whim, serving only jellied
cranberry sauce and two kinds of pie, neither of which is pumpkin.
        Away from her work and mine, ours is a surprisingly calm

and comfortable life of grocery lists, utility bills in the daily mail,
laundry, and laziness on Saturday mornings. And before she leaps
in costume and mask from our window, pursuing Truth, Justice, and

the American Way, she lifts on tiptoe and very carefully kisses me.

CRAVING
by Jo Angela Edwins

I can hear wise mothers
say it is the body's way
of crying out for what it lacks,
but there is more to this
than mineral deficiency.

Here the rigid scientist
can deny the soul,
but my bones alone
in their hunger for calcium
don't impel me to rocky road

any more than this animal
determined to project her DNA
accounts for the way I look at him—
his eyes turned and his hair mussed
as daylight slips through shadows.

There is a vibrancy to need,
the heart a perched bird
and the body a taut wire,
weariness and energy entwined,
a reminder we are alive.

Or like this: the fruit hangs
from the laden branch,
just out of reach.
We reach anyway, savoring
this wild electrical stretch.

COOKIE MAN AND THE SIX BOX LADY
by Chris Rodriguez

The last thing Cara needed at the start of her sugar detox was cookies. But, the doorbell rang again, and Robby asked from the top of the stairs, "Aren't you going to get that?" She tugged at her sweats, hung the resistance band over her shoulders, and reached the door before her son made it all the way down. She had seen the Brownie uniform through the sidelight window and instantly resolved to ignore the siren call. It was *that* time of year. Every spring, without fail, the cookies were planted everywhere. Store fronts, sidewalks downtown, in the park, and the fragrant boxes were even delivered right to your front step.

Cara opened the door and took a surprised step back when a man walked up behind the girl. The chaperone was generally a mother. She was disarmed by his rugged features. He gave her a shy smile and friendly nod. *Jeez!* A hand went up to push the sweat-soaked hair from her reddened cheeks. She nodded back, and though her lips tugged politely up at the corners, her smile could not break out through the clenched teeth of her humiliation.

"Buy some Girl Scout cookies?" the girl said with little hope. "So I can go to camp?" From the look of the heavy box her father held to his chest, they had either just started or hadn't had much luck in unloading the sweet treats.

"Yes!" Robby yelled from behind her. "We need some cookies, Mom. We haven't had any for a week," he told the girl. "Can you believe it? It's child abuse."

Cara's mouth stretched tightly. "Sorry," she addressed the man. "My son has bad manners. I'll get my wallet." She left the door cracked and dragged Robby over to plunk him firmly in a chair. "Just stay there, please. I'll buy one box, just one. Got it?"

Her purse was buried under the piles of mail on the credenza near the door. As she removed the debris and stacked it to the side, she heard the girl ask her father, "Daddy, can we go visit Mommy and take her some flowers today? I want her to see me in my uniform. She always loved it."

The man cleared his throat and replied, "Not this evening, Sweetie. Visiting hours are over. We'll go tomorrow. It's Saturday and we can spend a little more time with her, okay?"

"Sure, Daddy," the girl responded with obvious disappointment.

Cara felt her heart drop in her chest. *That poor family. Her mother must be very ill,* she thought as she reached back into her wallet and pulled additional bills from it.

At the door, she told the girl, "I'll take six. You pick for me." A glance up at the man rewarded her with a sincere look of appreciation as he lowered the box for his daughter to retrieve the cookies.

"One of each!" she said with exuberance. "Wow! That's the best we've done all evening, Dad!" He nodded and patted her arm at the good news.

"We sure appreciate it," he told Cara. "Come on, Ellie. Let's go get some dinner now. It's getting late and you have homework to do."

Cara watched as they trotted hand in hand down the walk, and her heart gave a little flutter when the man turned back to wave at her as they reached the car. *What a great father. You don't see that often enough these days.*

With her back to the closed door, she remembered the six boxes of cookies in her arms and responded to Robby's look of utter surprise. "I know, I know. I said one box. Guess you'll have to help me eat them." And at his "Yippee!" she reminded him, "After supper." She tossed the resistance band into the closet. *I don't know what I'm getting in shape for anyway. It's not like there's anyone special in my life.*

***

Though it was hot at the moment, Cara knew that as the sun sank lower in the sky, the temperature would drop considerably. She grabbed a heavy sweater and wrapped it around her waist. "Robby, don't forget your jacket!"

They were off to sell candy bars to fund Robby's Pee Wee Football League. His father had always taken the reins on this project in the past, but it was all up to Cara now. Wayne was gone, and she had become Robby's mother and father. It wasn't easy, but after nearly a year, she was at last working a routine into her own busy schedule. Lucky for her, she was able to work from home as an online grief counselor. She taught a few community education courses and presided over a support group as well, but was always

THE WAY TO MY HEART

able to be home with Robby and make sure he got where he needed to go. She felt it was important to keep to the schedule he was used to.

Two hours and six blocks later, they trudged up the walkway to a cute craftsman-style home. She could hear the drone of a vacuum cleaner inside. Cara stood back and let Robbie handle the encounter. He rang the doorbell, and when there was no answer, he rapped on the door. They heard the machine go silent and heavy footsteps approach. Robby took a step back to allow the storm door to open without hitting him. "Hello, I'm Robby," he started even before the person stood fully in the doorway.

Cara gazed in shock at the sight before her. It was the man who had come to her door with his daughter in the spring. A gingham apron covered the front of his distressed jeans. The fall colors of his plaid flannel shirt accentuated green eyes that fixed on Cara. A warm blush rose in her cheeks.

Robby stopped his scripted speech and looked from the man to his mother and back again. The man spoke. "The six-box lady!" he said in recognition.

Oh, great! Just what I want to be known as, she thought. No witty words came to mind in rebuff, so she just kept quiet.

"I was wondering if you wanted to buy some candy bars to help out my Pee Wee Football League," Robby started again. That broke the trance between them as the man held up a finger and turned to walk across his front room. It was a mess.

Cara chuckled as she remembered her first encounter with this man. *Payback's a bitch!* She watched as he tossed stuff from one pile to another on a counter top loaded with unfolded laundry. He pulled a cookie jar from the corner and grabbed a wad of bills from inside.

"I'll take six," he said with a wide grin as he jogged across the littered floor and handed the bills to Robby. "Sorry for the mess," he shot at Cara. "We're looking for a new housekeeper. Our old one got married."

She smiled back. "I understand," she said. "Happens to the best of us." Cara remembered the conversation between the man and girl when they were on her front doorstep. "How is your wife?" she asked politely.

The man looked up sharply at Cara. His brow furrowed. "My wife?" he questioned.

"Oh, I'm sorry if I seem nosy," Cara stammered. "It's just that I overheard your daughter asking if she could take flowers to her mother. I assumed she was ill."

"No." He went silent. Cara felt awkward and embarrassed that she had brought it up. She was only being polite. "She, um, passed away a little over a year ago," the man told her. "We were going to take flowers to the cemetery, but it was closed."

Cara was mortified. "I'm so sorry!" she managed. "I didn't know."

"Of course you didn't. Don't worry about it. It's okay." He looked back at his daughter as she sorted through toys on the floor. "We're okay," he told her.

Robby was looking back and forth between his mother and this man. When there was a break in the awkward conversation, he continued, "As soon as the order comes in, we'll deliver them to you. Thank you for supporting our fund-raising project."

The man smiled at Robby. "Payback's a b... uh, well you know, right?" he directed at Cara, who laughed at her own sentiment. He waved at the two of them as they headed back toward the street.

***

Cara finished up with her grief encounter support group and shoved papers into the tote beside her chair. The Cookie Man, as she had begun to think of him, popped into her mind. She wondered if she should mention her profession and invite him to a group or give him her business card at the very least. She had, in fact, thought of him often over the past few weeks. Not about his grief and loss, but about how he made *her* feel the two times they had seen each other. She hadn't felt that way about another man since she met her husband in college 15 years ago. It was both pleasant and weird at the same time.

"Grow up, Cara," she told herself. "You're not a school girl anymore."

***

A couple of weeks later, the candy bars arrived and were distributed to the parents to deliver. Cara would be grateful when this project was completed and they could move on to the next one—the upcoming holidays. Ugh! Although she tried to make them nice for Robby, it wasn't the same without Wayne. The family feeling had disappeared. Again, she wondered about the Cookie Man and his daughter. It must be difficult for them as well.

The fall weather had cooled considerably since their last visit to the cute little house. She and Robby were bundled up in jackets and heavy sweaters with caps on their flyaway hair. The brisk breeze swept leaves down the full gutters. Robby rang the bell, and they both stood back to wait.

The heavy front door flew open, and the man said, "Hurry, get in here before you blow away." He held the storm door open for them as they squeezed past. "Come on into the kitchen. We're carving a pumpkin for the front porch," he proclaimed with a gesture prompting them to follow.

"I'm Cara and this is my son, Robby," she told him. "We brought the candy bars you ordered." She scanned the room they stood in. The house was a lot neater than the last time Cara had seen it. No piles on the floor or clutter on the counters. "You must have found another housekeeper," she smiled.

"What?" he asked, then, "Oh, yes. We did, thank goodness. I'm the worst! I'm a contractor and built this house myself, but I sure can't keep it clean." He laughed at his incompetence. "Would you like some hot chocolate? I've got a pan on the stove already." He looked around at them as he grabbed mugs from a cupboard. "It will fortify you for the rest of your deliveries."

"Um, sure," Cara said as she looked at Robby, who had already headed to the table to help the girl yank the guts from the huge round gourd. It was his favorite Halloween activity. Cara felt a bit guilty that she hadn't bought him a pumpkin to carve and Halloween was only a week away.

"Hey, I'm Jack, by the way, and this is my daughter, Ellie." He ladled cocoa into the mugs and turned to hand her one. A blue streak of lightning sparked from his fingers to hers, and he almost spilled the contents of the mug as he jumped.

At the same time they said, "You shocked me!" then laughed. Cara glanced up to see his gorgeous green eyes and noticed they were directed at her bare ring finger. She reached to take the mug from him and offered, "My husband passed away not too long ago as well."

He nodded, took her by the arm, and led her to the table with Robby's mug in his other hand. "We seem to have a lot in common. I'd like to call you sometime soon."

As they sat in companionable silence while the children worked, Cara thought, *I think I'm going to need to get in shape to keep up with this guy. Never thought it would happen this fast.* She hid her grin inside the steamy mug.

THE RUM ANNIVERSARY
by Emily O'Neill

our first bar: a verb for a name
the perfect Lincoln Continental
parked in front & every glass / a face

puckered around pellet ice
I hated rum as a rule / from college
where they insisted / on ginger ale

to turn the spice vanilla
I'm not smart / as machete
blade falling through cane

unable to cull & process / what's sweet or worth
saving in a single day / me sweating
in your kitchen / before rum before

I imagined you / too particular
to kiss hungry / I called it *too much*
me / overwhelmed / it wasn't whiskey

for once & what's buzz / besides
blurring intention / I didn't
think you had a house at all

you / too kinetic to live
anywhere but in water rushing
past me / so I drank from sink tap

like a dog & dripped / under my dress
then took it off / only May
not the kind of day that boils

unless you leave the stove
so I walked away until
caramel bubbled three times its size

THE WAY TO MY HEART

stained pot bottom / dark
& maybe you're ginger
strung / through my stupid teeth

I need your need / louder
than my own breathing
when I say *use your words*

I need to believe you / still
in the room / your hands
remember me differently

than I deserve / cleaner
less hesitant / silly me / demanding
     a new love / leave the lights on

CHICKEN SOUP
by Lynn Hoffman

sanctify, complexify
brown the surface in hot fat
big pot, heavy like old age
make the meaty protein dance,
give up its brownings.
then get onions, carrots, caramel.
add layers and layers baby,
brown, brown, dark for later.
harvest, harvest, bring it home.
everybody in now: water, meat
garden stuff, garlic, sprig o'thyme

time to guard the gates
lower the heat, just simmer
slowly pull out the just-confected goods
no boil old girl, leave the
water-pipe mineral tang behind in the bones
keep the fat afloat above the water.

the meat's for the dog you know
the bit of salt's for old adam
and that little thing you put in the
bowl before you pour the soup?
the ginger thread, radish sheet
the english pea, the french green bean,
the oily mushroom rice, the scorched potato dice?
the finishing touch?
well that's just you sweetheart
just you today, pure you, eau de you.
that's the way you shake your shoulders
when they play the oldies or
that way you said "hello" and
that way you'll say "goodbye."

TELL ME HER NAME
by Judy Swann

Rex. Oh, for the love of Rex, whose likeness I craved the entire phlegmatic era of my youth, bulging shoulders, smooth triangle of his lower back. One day Rex sheathed my fourth finger in gold, bright and odorless. He is a farmer. He works the fertilizers all day, fiddles the gaskets of the cultivators, moves the sacks of seeds, centers the odors of clover, drives his tractor, stands in the grass. We live in a world of real home dinners—chili con carne, lamb fricassé, hot ham and hot peaches. His white man's neck and arms are the color of schoolhouse brick, his cheeks and eyelids are pistachio shells—black hair, black brows, green agate eyes. Rex. I am a nurse. I am the smell of formaldehyde and the tunnel white of hospitals everywhere, with the big thighs of a Mack cab and hands and cheeks the color of wheat. I make him sausage and Johnny cakes, a glass of ginger milk, and then I drive in to work. Every patient in the appropriate ward, like socks in one drawer, shorts in another. Some with cancer, some with fractures. We two are going on forty, and we have 50 acres. We eat together, and both of our parents are dead, as long ago now as seven years, as recently as March.

It is spring and Rex has been plowing it under, has been plowing under the old corn. "Catarina," he says to me, "the earth is a person." Katty, Kate, Reeny, and Ma. Rex names my two breasts, my two hands. Cattyree. My mouth. "Give me a kiss? Can I smoonch my head on you, Reeny and Ma?" Oh for the love of Rex, his twelve tough ribs and craggy wrists.

In Baxter General where I work, people die in cataracts. Spring floats them out by the dozens: old Milhaud of an infected tooth; Mrs. Zwiefel, lymphatic cancer; Anna Lamp's bleeding ulcer. I have a thyroid condition forever. They give me triiodothyronine; doesn't taste like much. Norma Hjalmson's piles are back, they won't kill her though. My skin is soft like a baby's. I simmer my Rex his apples and cabbage. I glaze his carrots with mustard. I nourish and tend as he nourishes and tends. We have only each other. The work weathers him hard and knotty. Me, I tend to fat. Rex puts his hands on my belly and laughs.

Knee high by the Fourth of July—every corn farmer says this—but Rex's is a good three feet. And not much foxtail. He manages the galinsoga in the spinach, puts copper on the tomatoes so they don't get blight. He's got some teenagers walking beans. It is 102° in the shade today. The elastic on my whites is shot; the seam is starting to give. Summer is the bloatingest time, the white of the year, sun blazing. Little Clara Zwiefel, her gut ballooning triumphantly with the leisurely lymph of disease, used to squeeze my hand and cry when Dr. Zaintz came with his needle, huge, like what they use on cattle, to siphon her off. It left a little hole in her navel, and when the pressure built up, she leaked. Zwiefel would stare at the ceiling and her eyes got blank and shiny, but she would ring that bell and I would come.

This now is like a bolt from the blue. It's 3:00 A.M. I'm a nurse and I'm still confused. I think it's my medicine, maybe early menopause. Or what I ate. It is August 11. Suddenly the bed is wet, my legs and Rex are wet. He is awake too all of a sudden. Is this indigestion? Bread salad with early hot peppers. I have the time to think about it. Maybe the juvie apples. I still don't know where the water is coming from. Rex makes the decision.

He drives me into Baxter; I am half myself. I think of Clara Zwiefel. There at Emergency, they lay me flat and wheel me in. I cry and ask them if they'll pump my stomach. My vulva burns. A miracle, a foot. Dr. Zaintz's nurse tells me I am giving birth. I am giving breech birth and the foot is just as big as the first joint of Rex's thumb. I am actually forty years old, a nurse, overweight, all right. I did not know. Past hope, I always thought. Can't you just take it out, I ask. Am I going to die? Will someone please anesthetize me?

The baby is the dull color of a piece of steak. All her parts are perfect. Whatever will we call her? Charlotte, Rosamund, Cuesta, Christa, Clio, Ra, Rachel, Rama, Robin, Rêves, so long as she lives. Russel, Reba, Consuela, Cynthia. In future memory to her doting parents. Signed with her own last name, perhaps? Liuba, maybe. Rosamund Liuba? What could be wrong with a nice nature name like Lentil or Lake? Cassy Lake is a nice name. Or really tough sounding names like Carp, Cod, or Reason? The baby has eyes like cloves and she smells of being inside.

Rex smells of worry; he is putty-colored and tired. I remember how he would come to me, freckles on his shoulders. Now he's hers. He holds her. He traces her tiny mouth with his pinky.

Will she still be here when I wake up? If I'm not dreaming, when I open my eyes, there will be a basket of laundry right here. It will have a receiving blanket in it and overalls. Rex?

FORTY-FIVE YEARS MARRIED, AND STILL, HE COOKS FOR ME
by Alice Morris

Pancakes a guy from Pennsylvania was flipping
      over a green *Coleman*
      the morning we first met at a hostel outside of Banff
      and I noticed
      his stunning blue eyes

Hot cross buns with bits of colorful citrus, and cup of bold
      at the bakery in Banff
      the first time I sat across the table from *the dude*
      who had been flipping pancakes
      and we gazed
      into each other's eyes

Six-layered shortcake–
      fresh strawberries, real whipping cream–
      our June wedding
      picnic lunch at conservatory–
      finger sandwiches, grapes, mangos, pomegranates, almonds,
      figs,
      and wine–
      aspen leaves rustling, air fragrant with scents
      of lily, fern, and rose

IT'S ALL IN THE TIMING
by Lynn Abendroth

5:30. *Just enough time*, Kay thinks, glancing at the clock on the stove, *to make biscuits*. The chicken, crackling in the oven, has just been given a splash of white wine.

With surgical precision, she scoops flour into the measuring cup, leveling it with a knife. One, then two cups go into the sifter. *Dan said he'd be home by 6:00*. With her job, the kids' activities, and the unpredictable demands of Dan's work, dinners together are becoming more and more scarce.

Taylor, dark eyes and dark hair, is nearly eight, but she is in a developmental time warp that traps her, physically and mentally, at about five. She stands at the sink, busy with her favorite dinnertime task, peeling carrots. She perches on a little wooden step stool that she carries from place to place.

Exactly three teaspoons of baking powder go into the sifter, followed by a teaspoon of salt and a bit of baking soda. Taylor turns to watch as the sifted flour rains softly down into a wide glass bowl. Kay passes the sifter to her, and she carefully taps out the last of it. "It's like snow," Taylor says, proud and smiling. She hands Kay the empty sifter and goes back to her carrots, a look of concentration returning to her face.

Edward sighs, exasperated by the fourth grade worksheet on the kitchen table in front of him. At ten, he hates math—hates school in general, in spite of his bright, inquisitive mind. Kay thinks, once more, of the irony. Edward has every gift, so much talent, yet he is always frustrated and negative. Taylor's cup, on the other hand, is always half full. She fully enjoys every moment—every event.

Kay thinks back on the serendipity that brought them all together. She'd been single for over a year when, at the end of a long day at her job at the Belle Patisserie, they had run into one another in the aisle at Trader Joe's. Literally. Dan had been pushing little Taylor in the cart and trying to walk toddler Edward by the hand when their carts collided. She smiles, remembering the comic scene, and how impressed she'd been by his calm patience. *His wife is a lucky woman*, she'd thought at the time, only to learn that his wife had died a few months before. A sweet year of talking, exploring, and falling in love had followed before they finally became a family. Now, these two feel just like her own—she calls them her gremlins—and she is determined to give them the love and stability they deserve.

5:45. Kay leans over Edward's shoulder, her blond hair brushing his dark brown, and looks at the worksheet, grimy with erasure marks, and offers a suggestion. She knows that he would allow her to do most of the work if she would, so there is a delicate balance between helping him and giving him the answers. His homework is a continual battleground of frustration for both of them.

"Why don't you take a ten minute break and ride your bike around the block? You know, clear out the cobwebs." She ruffles his hair, knowing that his return will bring exactly the same pattern. It is a cycle that seems to occur more and more often. It isn't that much homework, but by the time she cajoles Edward through it, it will have taken hours.

"Straight back, okay?"

He nods his agreement and rushes from the table, grateful for a brief reprieve.

5:59. Kay plops one third of a cup of combined shortening and butter over the sifted ingredients. With well-washed hands, she works it into small pieces—gently, but quickly so the butter doesn't get too soft. *Just right*, she thinks, wiggling her fingers to lose the last bits of dough. *This will be such a good dinner, and it's so important for us all to have this time together.* She knows better than to add the cup of buttermilk so soon.

The kitchen is suddenly quiet. Kay stands for a moment with her eyes closed, listening to the hollow ticking from the clock on the stove and the shoosh sound of the peeler against the carrot flesh.

She looks over at Taylor, who, by now, has peeled the carrots into needle-like orange stilettos. "Great job, sweetie!" Taylor's dark eyes shine, and she beams proudly. With Kay's help, she places some of the carrot shards into the salad and the rest into a plastic bag, where they will await their turn in the stockpot.

6:15. Kay pulls the chicken from the oven, setting the roasting pan on the cool side of the stovetop. Golden, juicy, perfect. *It can hold for thirty minutes*, she thinks, carefully tenting it with foil.

Edward comes back in, breathing hard. "That smells so good!" He edges close to the stove. "I'm starving!" *His mood has definitely improved.*

"Finish the worksheet, and by that time your dad should be here and we'll eat. And I'm making your favorite—biscuits!"

He flops reluctantly into the chair and hunkers over his paper again with a dramatic sigh. Kay pats his arm in encouragement and reaches for her phone. It won't hurt to call to find out how much longer, so she can make sure everything is timed perfectly.

No answer. Voicemail. Unusual. Dan always checks in. She recognizes the knot of minor annoyance that threatens to ramp into full-blown anxiety.

"Are you mad at me?" Taylor asks, her big dark eyes focused on Kay's face. Kay, surprised, turns to her. "Of course not, sweetie. You're my best helper. What makes you think I'm angry?"

Taylor looks into Kay's eyes and heart, searching for the right words.

"You've got that—that—*face look* on."

Kay sighs, hugging her. She is annoyed at her own transparency and, as usual, astounded by Taylor's intuitive read of the situation. *Face look!* Kay chuckles in spite of herself.

6:30. No sign of Dan—and no call. Edward works at his homework, while Taylor still hovers close to Kay, watching her every move.

6:45. Two pounds of potatoes, poached and tender, wait in simmering water. Kay empties them into a colander in the sink to drain. The rising steam bathes her face in heat, and she feels damp rivulets on her cheeks as she replaces the potatoes into the pan to dry their flesh before mashing. She starts Taylor crushing them with a hand masher, while she heats a small measuring cup of milk and butter in the microwave. *Wouldn't want the potatoes to cool too rapidly.*

7:00. *Surely he will be here any minute. Maybe he forgot to turn on his phone. May as well finish the biscuits.*

Kay adds the buttermilk with care, stirring the mixture until it is just blended. Hannah watches intently from the stool, knowing that any leftover dough will be hers to form. Kay turns the sticky dough onto a floured board, pushing it this way and that, tenderly, until it forms a soft, cohesive mass. Dipping a circle cutter first into the flour, she cuts twelve perfect shapes, which she places, sides touching, on a cookie sheet. *About ten minutes*, she estimates, watching as Hannah squishes and rolls the last scraps in her small hands, *to get those into a very hot oven.*

7:10. Kay puts the biscuits into the oven, then checks the chicken. It's still warm, but the juice is beginning to congeal. *No point in waiting any longer,* she decides, and begins carving it onto a platter.

"Good man!" she calls to Edward as he places the finished homework into his book bag and moves the place settings back into position. "Dad must have gotten held up at work, so let's just go ahead." The children happily take their places. Kay places the food on the table, and then goes back to the oven to remove the biscuits. Perfect! They are beautiful, golden, and light. She sits down, and they take one another's hands around the table. Edward says the blessing, then digs in. "May I have honey on my biscuit?" he asks, knowing that it is an indulgence not usually allowed. "Yeah, we want honey!" echoes Taylor, jumping on Edward's bandwagon.

They're interrupted by the grinding sound of the garage door opening. "I'm so sorry, baby; I had a last minute consult, then my phone died!" Dan rushes in, dropping his jacket on the hall post. "Wow! Something smells amazing!" Walking behind her, he plants a quick kiss on her neck before ruffling Edward's hair and kissing Taylor on the nose. Then he takes his place at the end of the table. "What a day! I'm so relieved to be home with my gremlins!"

"No problem. You're here now," Kay answers with a bright, bright smile. "Let's all have honey tonight!"

HAIKU
by Joanie DiMartino

humid night
we split a dish of iced lychees
catch each other's eye

HAIKU
by Joanie DiMartino

harvesting pawpaw
the rough of your hands
on my cheeks

ROSEMARY CHICKEN
by Jessica Abughattas

we can't help but dip our fingers in the pan
   taste   juices   lemon   lick our plates clean

we sip from our glasses as acid cuts
   caramel   thyme   tannins   swirl inside our mouths

I watch you tear meat with your teeth, hope
our lips taste like rosemary and syrah forever

is any flavor   a seat at any other table
as rare as lush   as maplewood   as us ?

we wash our hands
we smell dinner on our fingers for days

A PAIR OF MERRY MOLLUSKS
by Terri Elders

"A man taking basil from a woman will love her always."
-Sir Thomas Moore

February 14 fell on a Tuesday in 1956, not a good news day for us. Bob and I had hoped to spend our first Valentine's Day evening as a married couple at the Villa Nova, our favorite Italian restaurant. But I wouldn't get a paycheck until Friday, and we'd already spent Bob's GI Bill allowance on the rent and utilities for our tiny apartment.

"Don't worry, honey," Bob said that noon as we munched on our bologna sandwiches and apples on the shady patio of the cafeteria at Long Beach State College. "We'll celebrate tonight somehow."

An eternal optimist, Bob kept up the chatter as he drove me to the valve manufacturing firm atop Signal Hill. I'd been lucky in landing a part time job there, editing the company newspaper, a glossy monthly.

"I'll pick you up at 5:00. We'll have a cozy supper at home tonight. I think I'll have enough left after I fill up this old Pontiac's tank to buy a bottle of Chianti, and you can cook me up a Valentine's surprise."

It would be a surprise all right, I thought, trying to recall what remained in the pantry that I could make a meal of. Nonetheless, I forced a smile. At least we had each other, and we wouldn't be paupers forever. Bob intended to take the local police department exam in a couple of months, with the goal of joining the force by summer. We were certain he'd be assigned a swing shift, which would enable him to continue his police science studies at the college. He still had another year to complete for his degree.

At the office I conferred with Alisa, who worked in accounting.

"What can I make for a special supper tonight when I don't even have any meat?"

"Have you got any canned clams?"

"I think so, but that's hardly festive. Besides, Bob doesn't like chowder."

Alisa grinned. "I'm talking pasta, baby. Pasta means amore…trust me, I'm Italian. Men love pasta. I'll give you my mom's recipe. And remember, if you don't have one thing on hand, just substitute another. Santo Valentino would approve!"

"Saint Valentine's Italian?" I cocked my head and furrowed my brow. Somehow I'd vaguely thought of him as English, but realized I might have been thinking of a photo I'd seen of the statue of Eros in Trafalgar Square.

"Of course he's Italian! He's buried just north of Rome, near where my mom grew up."

Alisa scribbled down her recipe, and I tucked the folded paper into my pocket.

That evening Bob dropped me off at our place.

"OK, honey. You see what you can conjure up, and I'll go get gas and some wine."

I opened the recipe as I checked its ingredients against the few cans and jars remaining on the kitchen shelf.

Canned tomatoes, canned clams, olive oil, parsley, oregano, and my favorite, basil. Si certo, I had them all. Plus a package of linguini. I always kept onions and garlic on hand, and still had half a loaf of sourdough in the breadbox. I even had a shaker of grated Parmesan. We'd have a feast. I rummaged around and found a red and white checked tablecloth and a couple of candles to make our kitchen table even more festive.

We ate every bite, and Alisa was right. It indeed was the food of love. Bob sopped up the last of the sauce with the last of the bread and sighed.

"My compliments to the chef. But I can't keep eating all this pasta if I want to get in shape for the police exam," he said with a rueful shake of his head. He'd been running on the beach several evenings a week to prepare for the upcoming physical. "But tonight's special, so I think Saint Valentine will work his magic and make these calories not count."

"Did you know he's Italian?" I always liked to share my new knowledge with my amiable husband.

He looked at me as if I were demented. "What else would he be? What did you think?"

"Never mind." I sipped the last of my wine and smiled. "I'm just happy as a clam that you liked our dinner."

"And why are clams so happy?"

I was relieved he'd asked. I always enjoyed sharing such tidbits.

"People forget the second half of that saying. It's really 'happy as a clam at high tide.' I guess at high tide they are out there swimming around and not floundering on the sand where people dig them up."

"You're so smart," Bob said, laughing. "Wait right here while I get your Valentine's present."

He went into the bedroom and I heard him open a drawer. He came back with a homemade Valentine...a heart cut from the Sunday funnies, and a Hershey bar with almonds.

"Next year I promise a two-pound box of See's and a real Valentine," he said, giving me a hug.

"What do you mean? This is a real Valentine!" I opened it and read the verse he'd scribbled in crayon. Bob never had been noted for his poetic skill.

I read it aloud: "I will be your Valentine, if you will be my clementine."

I gave my husband a puzzled glance. "Clementine? Didn't she drown?"

"Clementine's the name for those little mandarin oranges we saw at the Piggly Wiggly last Christmas. Remember how juicy and sweet and squeezable they were?" He squashed my hand to make sure I got the picture. "And it's the only rhyme I could come up with at the moment for Valentine."

"I can think of another," I said, grinning.

"What's that?"

I giggled. "Frankenstein."

Bob hooted. "How about concubine? Or Palestine?"

We cleared away the supper dishes, merry as a pair of mollusks...at high tide.

Alisa's Mom's Pasta Amore

1 pound package linguini
1 tablespoon olive oil
½ cup chopped onion
1 tablespoon minced garlic
½ teaspoon crushed red pepper
2 tablespoons tomato paste
1 14.5 can tomatoes
2 6.5 ounce cans minced clams, undrained
1 tablespoon dried parsley
1 tablespoon dried oregano
1 tablespoon dried basil
salt, pepper to taste
Parmesan cheese, grated

Cook pasta according to package directions. Drain.

Heat olive oil in a large pot. Add onion, garlic, and crushed red pepper and sauté three minutes or until onion is browned. Stir in tomatoes and tomato paste. Cook until thick, stirring constantly. Stir in clams, parsley, oregano and basil. Stir until heated through. Serve atop drained pasta. Sprinkle with Parmesan cheese.

THE *BALL* JAR
by Mary Ellen Talley

I cling to you like the rubber rings on a canning jar.
Seal me. The noises of frustration overburden
fortune. Good fortune is in the eye of the beholder.
Behold the symptoms of optimal stair tread
creating friction on icy mornings. I warn you
tread lightly until traction on the mountain passes
tilts to switch seasons. You call this season empty/full,
a box with grosgrain ribbon tense for the curling.
The edge of curling's totally aware the present inside
is fragile. Wrapping paper around a glass gift
may be the most fragile instrument of power.
I empower you to grasp my circle. Although the rim
is smooth-ribbed metal, there's resistance enough
for you to grip the lid of the retro jar as you listen
for the pop of the seal. There are cling peaches inside.

SWEET BASIL
by Cameron D. Garriepy

"Andy, I literally couldn't have done this without you."

Her hair smelled like vanilla and lemon when she kissed his cheek. Five years, he'd worked for Kate Pease at her two locations—first in her downtown pastry shop, then as a manager at her café at Cooper Vineyard—and every day of those five years he'd slept with that distinctive scent in his dreams.

Kate's husband (because of course if you're going to nurture an unrequited passion for your boss, she should be blissfully married) was launching his latest novel at Kate's vineyard café in—Andy checked his smartwatch—fourteen minutes, and so far he'd kept a handle on every detail.

"No problem, Kate. We're all really happy for Ewan."

Kate swept away, the swishy folds of her skirt brushing up against the long legs he'd admired since he was a college freshman.

"She's too old for you."

He hadn't seen Danny—*Danielle*, he mentally corrected himself, she was going by Danielle now—in weeks, not since she'd gone back to school after spring break, but there she was beside him, a tray of bud vases for the buffet tables perched on her shoulder. She was right, but that didn't mean he didn't fall in love with Kate again on a daily basis.

"Shut up, Danny."

"Whatever." She shrugged and continued past him.

She'd cut her hair short and dyed it platinum blond since her last shift. He'd liked it long and dark, especially the secret shocks of violet you only saw when she put it up, but this suited her, too.

"Andy?" Margot, who ran the downtown location, peeked out from the kitchen. "Can I borrow a couple of staffers? I need to bring the cake in from the van."

"Sure thing, Margs."

And just like that, it was show time. Kate was counting on him.

Events meant keeping his head in the game, but two hours in without a hitch meant he could step back and breathe. He paused by the bar to survey the room, his eyes lingering on Kate, who swayed with her husband on the rented dance floor.

Danny wove through the tables collecting empty glasses, stopping to deposit her tray on a folding stand nearby. She elbowed him playfully, following the direction of his gaze. "If we weren't such good friends, I'd say something about how good they look together."

He eyed the tray of glassware.

"Yeah, yeah. I know." She hoisted the tray. "You coming out after?"

He shrugged, but Danny was already pushing through to the kitchen. He looked at his watch. An hour to go.

Kate always stopped in the kitchen to say goodnight to the staff after a function, and tonight was no different. He watched her depart, hand-in-hand with her husband, and wished desperately for his other vice.

Satisfied that Margot had a handle on things, he slipped out into the vineyard and down to the dock the owners kept for summer lake traffic.

He let his legs dangle over the edge, lit a cigarette, and listened to Lake Champlain lap at the wood beneath him, knocking his ashes carefully into a paper cup.

He could hear footsteps on the dirt path above. He'd thought the vines hid him from view, but he hadn't counted on Danny.

"Those things are gross. Girls won't want to kiss you."

"Jeez, Danny, are you thirteen?"

"It's a good thing you're grandfathered in. People call me *Danielle* these days." She plunked down next to him. "And I'm twenty-one, as you well know. You were at my birthday party."

She'd thrown back every shot anyone bought her, including an ill-advised round of schnapps. He'd held her hair back while she threw up in the ladies' room, and then driven her out to Fuller's Dairy, where she stayed when she was home from school. She'd changed all his radio presets, but she hadn't puked in his car.

"How did you know I was down here?"

She wiggled her fingers like a sideshow mystic. "I see everyyythinggg."

"Weirdo." He put out a hand to nudge her, but the playful gesture felt wrong somehow.

"I saw you attempt a subtle exit after Margot clocked us out. When you didn't come back, I figured you were hiding, or you finally drowned yourself because Kate Pease is still married to Mr. Tall Dark and Broody."

"Nice, Danny." He rubbed out the cigarette, dropping the butt into the cup. Burning down his place of employment—or the terraces of Marquette and Frontenac grapes—wasn't on his to-do list for the evening. "Don't you have someone else to torture?"

"Actually, no." She tilted her head and batted her lashes. "And I need a ride."

He sighed. Danielle Beaudette was not a flirt, but her thick, black cat-eye makeup and sooty eyelashes made a convincing argument in her favor nonetheless.

"Come on." He hoisted himself up and grabbed his soaking filter, swimming in its cup. "For all you know, I have a hot date to get to after I drop you off with the cows."

Danny laughed heartily at his back all the way up the hill to the staff parking lot, but she was uncharacteristically quiet during the ride out County Road.

"You okay?"

She tucked her hair behind her ear, her face deeply shadowed in the dark car. "Yeah. Just thinking."

He swung into the Fullers' driveway. The farmhouse was dark, except for a light in the kitchen window.

She gathered up a grimy messenger bag from the floor of his car. "You want to come in? I didn't eat before the party, so I'm going to make some food."

He thought of the older couple who owned the farm. "I don't want to impose."

"Oh, Walt and Molly are next door tonight visiting their grandbaby." She opened the car door, climbed out, then leaned back in. Andy couldn't help appreciating a brief view of unexpected lace and curved flesh. "So?"

He *was* hungry. "Can you cook?"

"Enough to feed myself."

He killed the engine and followed her to the back porch. She fished out keys, let them in, and pointed him to a basket of slippers before unlacing her black combat boots, toeing off her socks, and sliding her feet into a pair of green suede moccasins. "Molly doesn't like shoes in the house."

He poked around until he found slip-on fleece house shoes that sort of fit and shuffled after Danny, through a cozy den, and into the kitchen.

Danny was already banging around. She'd pulled out a cast iron skillet, some bacon, and a loaf of Sweet Pease honey-oat sandwich bread.

"BLTs?"

It struck him as odd, seeing Kate's bread on someone's counter. He'd made countless sandwiches at work over the years, but rarely considered that people who bought whole loaves might do the same.

"Earth to Andy?" Danny rapped on the skillet with a pair of tongs, then waved at him with them. "Can you stop thinking about the boss for four seconds and open that cabinet? Plates."

A violent flush rose up his neck. "I wasn't—"

"Thinking about Kate? Liar. Your face gets all weird when you do." She rolled her eyes back and let her jaw go slack.

He fetched the plates, and then reached for the single tomato resting on the windowsill. Danny laid the bacon out in the hot pan, and handed him the serrated knife from the block by the stove top.

He sliced the bread, then the tomato, thick like he would have for a customer. "Toaster?"

Danny kicked at a lower cabinet door. The toaster was inside on a shelf, its cord coiled around it.

He had to cram the bread in a little, but he got the toaster going. Danny was flipping bacon. The kitchen smelled amazing.

Andy opened the fridge, looking for mayonnaise, and found the jar on the door. What interested him more was a stack of glass storage containers. There was a beautiful collection of cheeses in those containers.

"Are we allowed to eat the cheese?"

Danny laughed, pulling the last slice of bacon from the pan. The toast popped. "Yes. Look." She slid the skillet off the burner to cool and wiped her hands on a kitchen towel. "I live here. Walt and Molly stepped in and offered me a place with them when things at home were…not good. This is the place I think of when someone says home. If we want to eat the cheese, we eat the cheese."

While Danny started assembling sandwiches, Andy pulled together a plate of cheeses. He glanced back at Danny, who had laid the sandwiches out open-faced. "Where's the lettuce?"

"Still in the garden."

She picked up the plate with the sandwiches, reached into the fridge for a glass bottle of milk, and breezed past him.

"Where are you going?"

"Bring the cheese. We're going to get the lettuce."

He tromped after her, delayed by changing back into his shoes. Her slippers lay abandoned by the door, but so too were her heavy, black boots.

He'd expected a practical vegetable patch. Instead, Danny waited for him on a whimsical bench fashioned from what looked like driftwood, amidst a maze of trellises and raised beds. A lush jungle of edibles slept in the blue darkness. Andy smelled damp earth and growing things.

He recognized Danny in that scent. This garden, it was hers.

"You got any basil out here?"

She laughed, pointing to a nested stack of round pots. "Over there. Top tier."

He wound his way between the beds. Pea vines, leafy bean bushes and taller climbing squashes, blossoms closed against the night. Flowers were artfully tucked in with the food.

"Did you do all this?"

Danny's voice floated back to him. "Sort of. There's always been a kitchen garden here. Since before Walt was born. He and Molly have helped me with building the boxes and stuff, but yeah. It's what I do, or at least what I want to do."

He often forgot that about her, since he only saw her at work, or when the Sweet Pease gang went out after hours. She'd worked at Coulson's nursery, too, before starting college, and still did in the summers. He pinched off a handful of sweet basil leaves and brought them back to her on the cheese plate.

"Better than plain old lettuce."

She shook the dew off the leaves and spread them on the sandwiches, patting the bench next to her. Her feet were bare, toes curling into the stone and dust.

It was only just dark enough for stars thanks to the late summer sunset. He let the living quiet settle over him while he tucked in. The valley chorused with peeper frogs and crickets, the occasional car or truck on County Road, and the barely perceptible sleep-sounds of the dairy herd.

"You were right about the basil." Danny set down what remained of her sandwich and scooped up a bit of soft cheese with her finger. "I hope you don't mind my fingers in the food."

He didn't, now that she mentioned it. "We did eat unwashed basil."

"Unwashed basil, fingers in the cheese. We are adventurers." She licked her finger. "That's really good."

He didn't want to be intrigued by her bowed lips and her fine-boned hands that were always slightly chapped, at odds with her pin-up girl makeup and ever-changing hair.

"I've been paying attention to the vendors."

"Impressive, since Kate's usually around for that."

He set his plate down too hard, nearly sending his half-eaten sandwich into the gravel path. "You never let up. What is it to you if I like Kate?"

She leaned back and leveled him with a cool look that reminded him that she wasn't just the sarcastic kid Margot had hired a couple of years back. "Maybe I don't want to see you miss opportunities while you're pining for someone who is never going to feel that way about you."

"Yeah." His laugh turned bitter. "Like who? It's not like I've ever been a girl magnet."

Danny pursed her lips—with a healthy dose of side-eye—and returned to eating her sandwich, snagging a slice of another cheese and sliding it between the bread slices as she did.

Andy left his food, the bench, and Danny's infuriating snark and wandered into her garden. Through the firs ahead, he could make out the shadowed silhouette of the grand Victorian house next door. Around a corner of the building, he could just see the flickering glow of firelight, and if he stretched out his ears, he could hear laughter and low music.

Kate—and her husband—might very well be there. The owners were her friends.

"I lived there for a while when I was younger."

Danny's voice was soft—wistful—and he felt sorry for taking a verbal swing at her.

"I didn't know that."

"My mom was Meg Swift's home health aide before they moved to be closer to her grown kids. They let us stay in the apartment over the garage." He hadn't heard her get up, but she appeared next to him among her plants. "I was always happy there. I mean, I was a teenage jerk to my mom, and I had stupid taste in boys, but things didn't get bad until we moved in with my uncle."

Andy slung an arm around her, hugging her to his side. "You seem happy here, though."

She shifted slightly, leaning into him a little. He liked the way she fit there.

"I am. I have better taste in men now, too."

He wondered who the lucky guy was just as he realized he was holding another guy's girl, then let his arm drop away.

"You're not even going to ask."

He turned at the sharp wonder he heard. Her expression was fierce, her body suddenly rigid with tension.

"You, you idiot."

Him, what? He had just enough time to blink before she stretched up and kissed him full on the mouth. She let her lips linger for a beat against his; his body responded before his head could catch up.

He caught her arms, sliding his hands down to hold her hands, leaning in to let the kiss play out between them.

She tasted of basil leaves. Her skin was impossibly soft, right down to her palms, but he could feel the calluses on her fingers. The scent of earth and rain clung to her like perfume.

She rocked back on her heels, pulling away from him but holding him in her gaze. "You."

He reached up to touch her cheek, and she pressed her face into his hand. The gesture was so unabashedly tender, so unlike Danny. A pang of longing squeezed his chest.

"I didn't know." He whispered it, feeling every inch the idiot she'd called him.

Danny tightened her hold on his other hand. "Now you do."

RED WINE
by Steve Cushman

We spent that winter sampling red wines,
some we liked but most we didn't.
Neither of us had ever been wine drinkers
I preferred beer; margaritas were your thing
but we'd read the reports about the health
benefits of red wine and both approaching
fifty decided it was time to try. Each night
we'd drink a glass and sometimes two
discuss the flavors as if we knew what
we were talking about: *too dry, too sweet,
too bubbly,* both of us wondering what we were
doing, both of us happy, after twenty-seven
years of marriage, to try something new.

EXCESS IN PARIS
by Gretchen Fletcher

where after sex we wrapped ourselves
in Porthault robes, ate gift basket pears,
and stepped through French doors onto the balcony
where we could look into that designer's atelier
and down on the *Rue de la Tremoille* where
someone was always playing "La Vie en Rose"
while we watered geraniums
with little green bottles of Perrier,
an excess, yes,
but you had to be there, I guess.
It seemed to make sense at the time.
There was so much of Paris,
and we didn't want to waste a drop of it,
wanted, instead, to use it up,
and order every morning
those little melons with heart-shaped tops
and piles and piles of *fres du bois,*
then at night suck powdered cocoa
off fistfuls of those almonds from Les Princes
before making love again.

THE WAY TO MY HEART

HARRY & DAVID'S ROYALE RIVIERA PEARS
by Katherine Edgren

*After years of study, scientists discovered
pears are best eaten naked, in the bath,
their juices streaming down.*

They came in the mail.
As per pear instructions,
we waited—only two days—
and they were ready.

Blessed with a perfect moment of just-ripeness.
Vigilance is required to discern the instant in its thinness.
Best when it all comes together—texture, flavor,
when just the right notes sing.

Each day we remembered to check back,
to open the dark box resting on the counter
and fingertip-test where the stem joins the fruit—
the fontanel of the pear.

With such fleeting perfection,
each pear joins the society of others with too-short lives—
the mayfly, the day lily, the evening primrose.

Cool and sweet, white-fleshed and plush;
good thin-sliced, with alternating bites
of sharp white cheddar on a fresh plate,
juicy snowflakes drifting outside.

The pears are voluptuous.
Dimpled, they blush and turn,
open and open again.
The cool shell softens, lingers,
and like love, there's ripening, yielding.

We both inhale.
Our hands, mouths, tongues, lips
find, nibble, bite, catch

the succulence, as we abandon ourselves
to the sweetness of submission.

SLICE OF LIFE
by Julia Tagliere

Corporate holiday gift baskets, as a rule, are depressing: bottles of mediocre red wine; diminutive cardboard boxes full of communion-wafer crackers; and, inevitably, a shrink-wrapped brick of cheese-like substance, the criss-cross stripes of its rubbery beige rind like pale scars—all festively cellophaned and tied with a gaudy bow. Happy Holidays from our Human Resources Department to you…well, you humans.

This basket, however, was different. It had already been opened, for one thing, which is generally not the custom in our family; we prefer to leave them unopened until at least March, then humanely dispose of the contents. The other thing was the way in which my husband swept into our kitchen like a conquering hero, placed the basket on the counter with a flourish, and immediately pulled out a chunk of something crumpled inside a cocoon of plastic wrap. He danced straight to the silverware drawer for a knife. "You *have* to try this."

Allow me to say, at this point, that I do not possess an adventurous palate. My husband knows this and, in the past, has successfully used "You have to try this" as a means of forcing me to try shifty-looking quasi-edibles by deploying the phrase in front of our children, whom we're trying to raise to be "good little tryers." Thus, I eyed the plastic chrysalis in his hand with some misgiving.

"What is it?" I suspiciously watched him peel the layers of wrapping from the mass. Through the opaque plastic, I began to see smeary glimpses of verdant green, like moss through a foggy window.

"What *is* it?" He removed the last of its filmy cocoon and held it out triumphantly for me to see. "It's cheese." I looked skeptically at the large wedge he cupped reverently in his hands: it was surprisingly beautiful. The rind revealed was more emerald in color; the cheese itself was firm and a milky white, alabaster flesh untouched by the sun. I leaned a little closer and gave a small sniff, still not quite trusting my husband's motives. Was this, perhaps, Limburger in disguise?

As I inhaled its fragrance, my fears dissolved. My mouth watered convulsively. Its perfume was pungent, richly infused with an almost palpable creaminess and a tartness I could not define. I felt the first stirrings of hesitant desire. I looked up and nodded to my husband: I would, indeed, try. He eagerly and tenderly coaxed a small, crumbly morsel from the wedge and placed it on my waiting tongue. Its tanginess penetrated the tender buds on the tip of my tongue as the velvety white flesh melted in my mouth. Delicate crystals shivered their way across my teeth. I closed my eyes, lost in blissful, gustatory communion. I swallowed the last glorious swallow with a feeling of profound sadness at the emptiness of my mouth. Without opening my eyes, I said, "More. Please." My husband happily obliged, granting me another precious mouthful, a dewy milk pod bursting open on my tongue and flooding my mouth with delight. Fairly purring now, I sank into a chair and sighed contentedly. "What is this and where can we get more?"

He joined me at the table, carving off, I noted, a quite *large* slice for himself; my eyes narrowed as I visualized the tipped scales of his portion as compared to mine. "Isn't it good? I don't know what it's called," he blithely replied, gobbling his entire slice down in one hedonistic gulp. The briny kiss of this new love still tingling on my lips, I felt the beginnings of panic start to rise. "What do you mean, you don't know? Where did you get it? What store did they buy the basket from?" As my husband unconcernedly chopped off yet another enormous *tranche* for himself, I began tearing apart the rest of the basket, searching frantically for a store label. There was none. Typical corporate holiday gift basket, I thought bitterly. I sank back into my chair, dejected.

"What's the matter? Don't you like it?" My husband was blissfully unaware of my sense of loss at realizing that this rapidly shrinking wedge was all that remained of such ecstasy. I felt the desolate sensation of two ships having passed in the night.

Seeing my husband raise the knife once again, I moved quickly and grabbed the remaining treasure, hurriedly, but lovingly, cocooning it once again in its cradle of plastic wrap. "Why don't we save this for later? Maybe this weekend get a good bottle of wine to go with it?" My voice sounded artificially cheerful, even to me. "Okay," my husband said over his shoulder as he left the kitchen to change out of his work clothes, innocent of my machinations.

After watching him retreat down the hallway, I gazed in wicked, adulterous triumph at the surprisingly weighty jewel I now held in my hands, knowing full well that this weekend, the good bottle of wine would be consumed *sans fromage*—at least, sans *this* fromage. I hid my stolen, anonymous love deep in the refrigerator, behind the plain yogurt (where I knew it would be safe). I dreamed of the midnight *rendez-vous* to come.

THE DECADE MENU
by Teresa De La Cruz

think and search through the last ten years…
so much has been served, but a certain few are worth cheers

PECORINO SMOKED ON A BARREL PLANK with FIGS
and TOASTED PISTACHIOS
a deconstructed first kiss drizzled in honey
where pinot noir smoke fills the cave like a rustic home
and the figs last as long as the heart beats

SALMON CHOWDER
subtle pink flesh swims to a flourish
and a spoon is a spear is a scoop
the color of a soft sunrise

CEVICHE with ROASTED PINAPPLE, AVACADO
and PLAINTAIN CHIPS
there is a market for sunlit skin, cilantro, and zest.
it cruises in and out of bays, then lingers tropical
to trigger and treat

THE FRIED CHICKEN OF YOUR DREAMS
so divine and only for night
with crisp and crackle that requires no eye contact
or polished teeth, for the biscuit and honey
will dwell very, very well

QUARK MOUSSE with POACHED BLUEBERRIES
and CANDIED BUCKWHEAT
quiver and query through the liberty of sweet
as Dali brush strokes berries atop the perfect combination
of quark cream, vanilla, and crunch

ON BAKING, RELATIONSHIPS, ETC.
by Marta Ferguson

You can blow it if you try too hard.
The dough needs only so much
flour, water too, but you'll throw
it off if the recipe, which ought
to guide you, grinds you into
some cookbook-led convert,
convinced it's got to be this way.

Let it be its own way, sated with
rye flour and a little all-purpose,
instead of flakes or bricks, make bread
that rises of its own accord, that needs
less help from you.

THE TAGINE
by Susan McGee Bailey

The rusty-orange earthenware contraption with its cone-shaped cover sits on top of my refrigerator. Traces of blackened food dot the lip of the platter, the rim of the cover. Rather than a thing of beauty, this Moroccan tagine strikes visitors as nothing more than a well-used cooking pot.

But I was never the one to use it. It is out of place in a kitchen lacking other evidence of food preparation: no copper pans, no Cuisinart, not even a coffee maker. Yet the tagine has crowned this refrigerator and the one before it and the one before that ever since the summer day in 1993 when I'd lugged it home from Brussels in my carry-on bag. The oversized vessel was a gift from Jean, my lover of several years. He had insisted. "Suzanne, you must haves it, to eat well and to thinks of me in your kitchen!"

Our affair began in 1982, two strangers exchanging smiles across a Washington, D.C. dinner table. The evening was one of the few times I'd left my eleven-year-old daughter without hesitations. A friend who had trained as a nurse was visiting, and she understood Amy's disabilities. No tears to steel myself against, no sudden clutch in my stomach as I left for the dinner party—only the lightness of undiluted anticipation.

I had just turned forty. Jean was divorced, in town from Brussels on a short assignment for the World Bank. Neither of us had paid particular attention to the other before dinner as we sipped Pisco Sours and talked with several South American guests. When the meal was served we were seated at opposite ends of the table. Then, as I laughed at a story being told by our host, I noticed Jean smiling toward me. I returned his smile. For a few seconds our eyes locked. In an instant I took in his hazel eyes and red-blond hair as it curled around one ear. Jean picked up his wine glass and nodded toward me before drinking. After dinner we sat side by side in the living room. I hadn't smoked in years, but when he offered me a cigarette, I smiled and leaned toward him for a light.

The following summer I flew to Brussels, met Jean's friends, his ex-wife, and his two children. Over several bottles of wine we planned our trip. The children would drive with us from Brussels, down through the Loire Valley, and on to the Club Med in Cadequez on the Spanish coast. I would stay a day or two in Cadequez, then take the train to Barcelona, see the city, and fly home. Fourteen-year-old Patrick was perpetually annoyed with his father. He lectured Jean on the dangers of smoking and hated his drinking. "Please, Suzanne, you tell him, no more wine! Please!"

At twelve, striving for sixteen, Anouk was moody and unhappy. It was obvious she viewed me as a rival for her father's attentions. Jean was oblivious. He eventually agreed to moderate his drinking at lunch, but would not go along with my suggestion that Anouk, Patrick, and I take turns sitting beside him in the front seat. "No, no, the childrens in the back, on that I am decided!"

Anouk had long, titian hair. I admired it and asked her to show me how to fix mine like hers: flowers behind her ear, wavy locks flowing over one shoulder. "*Oui*, Suzanne. You so *Américaine*, no *élégance*. My way for Europe!"

She glowed with pride when Jean agreed. "*Mais oui*, Anouk. Much better hair for Suzanne!" When we reached Cadequez, Barcelona faded. I stayed with Jean and the children until the morning of my flight home.

For the better part of the next fifteen years Jean and I made the most of stolen moments: summer visits to Europe when Amy went to a special camp in West Virginia, an occasional day or two when he flew into Washington or New York for meetings, a memorable New Year's Eve in St. Lucia, and once, four sultry August days in Anguilla. The island was devoid of tourists. The empty beaches shimmered in the sun as we strolled along the water's edge, savoring the sensuous scrub of wave-worn shells against our feet. Now and then we stopped to chat with fishermen, examined their catches, and one day bought a large fish. "Ah, I needs my *tajine* to makes this fish more special, Suzanne! But this will do—fresh food in our little cottage by the sea!"

Tagine meals signaled Europe and summer. And Jean. I loved the tantalizing scents of his *tajine de poulet* as it simmered on the gas burner: chicken, lemon and olives, traces of cumin, turmeric, maybe some cinnamon mixed with ginger. I loved the cool, crisp taste of white French burgundy on my tongue and in my throat while I gazed at Jean bent over the stove. In the hot, tiny kitchen his gradually graying hair, damp with perspiration, curled against his neck as he cooked. "Fresh, Suzanne, always only fresh herbs from the *petit* pots. You hears me?"

I delighted in the last minute hustle: a salad still unmade, the business of finding the correct wine glasses, often a ringing phone signaling additional guests. Jean's garret above a farmhouse outside Brussels fit four, could squeeze in six *à table*. We were often eight or more. On those occasions we needed to reorganize, serve buffet, sit on cushions.

"Ah, Suzanne, like Morocco, *parfait*, and you handles the bed, make it like, how you say? A couch, *oui, un grand* couch, *parfait!*"

I even loved the sounds of Jean's friends arriving. Vibrations, creaky steps, happy voices floating up the narrow winding staircase. Garbled greetings, warm embraces, French and English twisted through each phrase. "*Voici*, here we are, *on est la!*"

"*Suzanne, Jean, pret?* Ready now?"

"*Non? How you say, Suzanne?* No problem? *Oui*, no problem, *nous avon* with wine, *beaucoup de bon vin!* Much good wine!"

My welcome dinner to Belgium had become a tradition now, after several summers. For two weeks each August I shape-shifted from a single mother with a disabled daughter and a demanding career to a younger version of myself: blond hair loose down my back, clothes a tad too revealing for my stateside life, a bikini and fancy underwear in my suitcase. The two weeks flew by, but this was never considered. I closed my mind to all but the moment.

Jean never failed to ask about Amy, to empathize with my anguish over each new surgery her disabilities required. On the rare occasions when the three of us were together in the States, Jean and my daughter were easy and loving together. They played Slap Jack and he read *Peter Rabbit* out loud. "*Petit Amiée* likes bunnies. No?"

Amy always laughed. "No say me 'no'! Amy *likes* bunnies! Say me 'yes'!"

Sometimes weeks after any mention of him, she would ask, "Mother, where is that so nice man who say words so funny? Will he come see us soon? Tomorrow? Next week?"

The silver Moroccan bracelet Jean sent years ago no longer fits Amy's adult wrist. That it's too small is of no importance to my daughter. She's left the bangle in its place on her bureau. I smile each time I see it.

A romantic and a hedonist, Jean was incapable of a settled life. I was leery of commitments. His ex-wife and I became friends. Their marriage had faltered in the wake of mutual affairs. I understood the lingering bonds of a failed marriage, of children. She understood I posed no threat to their relationship. She posed none to ours. Together with her lover, the four of us sometimes vacationed together. My friends considered my relationship with Jean unusual, too fragile to last. But neither Jean nor I harbored illusions of fidelity. He had little interest in my life when we were not together. I insisted only on an absence of deceit and found his tales of various adventures and entanglements more entertaining than upsetting.

Jean's life was extreme—disorganized, hectic, but with ample time for friends, for wine, and women. He introduced me to the importance of vacations, the joy of impulsive decisions, and the positive side of overindulgence. A doctor of tropical medicine, he traveled to various parts of Africa five or six months a year, consulting for the World Health Organization and the World Bank on maternal-child health, the prevention of HIV/AIDS. The work was draining, often discouraging. He called me at odd hours—from Rabat, Abidjan, Kinshasa, a late night party in Brussels. "Suzanne, what time has you? Ah, so early morning and you awake? You works too much, *mon amour*!" He escaped the 1994 genocide in Rwanda by hanging onto the underside of one of the last UN trucks to cross the border. His 6:00 a.m. call from Tanzania was brief. "*C'est moi*, Suzanne! I arrives here safe, I see you soon, maybe? Now I run to catch the Belgium plane. Big kiss!" I hadn't even known he'd been working at a clinic in Kigali.

Perhaps the only shared expectation we had of each other, I think now, was one of permanence.

We celebrated New Year's Eve in 1997 at Jean's newly purchased *riad* inside the old city gates of Marrakech. Five days were all I could manage, but I had accumulated enough frequent flyer points. His mother, his ex-wife, and her mother would all be there. Patrick and Anouk were grown now, a decade and a half since our trip to Cadequez. They had friends of their own. "Come, Suzanne, hops the plane! Join the family! Why not?"

Jean and I scoured stalls in the *souk* for just-right furniture. We ate delicious lunches on the sunny roof top terrace as the call to prayer rang out across the city. The lamb or chicken tagine dishes with couscous were each delicious and different. Their spicy fragrances rippled in my mouth, then lodged in the wrinkles of my brain. In the cool evenings, wrapped in shawls, we drank champagne in the lantern-lit inner garden and watched the chameleon Jean had rescued. Its tail had been severed when dead branches were removed from trees in the courtyard. The chameleon could not navigate down the trunk of the lemon tree. The small creature made its home in a basket of tropical fruit for a day or two, then disappeared.

Jean was happy and excited as we planned new lighting and plantings, but seemed to tire easily. One afternoon he had a bad headache. When I asked, he laughed and made jokes. "You keeps me up at night, Suzanne." I laughed with him. I didn't comment on how quickly he slept as his head hit the pillow.

Early one morning the following March the phone rang. *"C'est moi,* Suzanne! I survives!"

"What, Jean? What did you survive?"

"Ah, *mon amour,* I decide better you not worry, I not tell you. They opens my brain and gets the tumor. Very uncertain, but okay now. We plan for the summer, no?"

With friends in London we talked of renting a place in the Greek Islands. I would fly first to Brussels, visit with family and friends, and then Jean and I would fly on to Greece. I confirmed the plans, made plane reservations. But by August it was clear Jean could not go on to Greece. When I arrived in Brussels he was at home—thin, the gray curls I loved gone, poisonous transfusions coursing through his body every few hours. Lifelong friends from medical school hovered nearby, their skills devoted to two goals: keeping Jean out of the hospital and maximizing the chances the aggressive treatments would slow the cancer. The brain tumor had not been the primary site. Jean had advanced kidney cancer. They told me there was a chance, but only a slim one. "He needs hope, Suzanne. He must have every hope. Medicine is the mind and the drug."

Body odors no one else could detect made him nauseous. "Ah, Suzanne, you has come. Sits beside me. You smells okay. And you smile. Now you will tell me the truth. You, you who says me always, 'just tell me the real story, Jean, no rounds about.' You I trust. Am I going to die?"

I knew the words I had to say. Looking into his eyes, I willed a smile. "Would I be flying on to Athens if I thought you were dying?"

Later, outside on the lower terrace, one of his friends reached for my hand. "Suzanne, when Jean first told me of you years ago, he said, 'You will like her, so *Américiane*—looks so *ingénue,* so innocent. Don't be fooled.'"

I wasn't sure how to react, not certain of his point. I turned to him with a questioning look. I tried to summon a smile.

"I see you understand you must go to Greece. Only that will give him hope." He squeezed my hand.

I abandoned my attempted smile. "I know."

For the next few days I helped family and friends with Jean's care and busied myself with household tasks. More friends appeared every evening. They prepared meals while I organized an outdoor table. Jean sat with us when he could, wrapped in blankets, shivering in the warm sun. He was unable to sip our ice-cold champagne, or taste his favorite tagine meals, but his spirits were undaunted. "Ah, *mes bons amis*, we lives the hours!"

I looked away. I had to continue what I had begun. I had to leave.

Each day I called Jean from a phone booth on the tiny Greek island where several of us had rented a cottage. I shared greetings from our friends and spoke of the sun, the salty sea, the stars in a jet-black sky.

The poisons did their work. By October Jean was in remission. On the phone he was jubilant. "I has nine lives, Suzanne! You flew away, and I knew you said me the truth!" He completed a report for the World Bank and planned a brief visit to Marrakech, then a trip to the States in March. The Moroccan visit was extended. "Suzanne, seems I am so busy. I comes a little later, *mon amour,* in June. We has to plan champagne, a special fête for the birthday of Suzanne!" In early April, another call came from Marrakech, Jean's son's voice on the line. I didn't need to hear the words.

The rough terra cotta pot is heavy, cold, and hard to the touch on the rare occasions when, cleaning the kitchen, I lift it down from its perch. Preparing the sweet, spicy tagine meals wasn't something I ever did. My role was to share the delight, hold the memories, participate in putting away one reality and escaping into another for a little while.

Now the food-crusted cooking pot contains chocolate I hope to conceal from Amy when she is home on weekends, the sea salt kettle chips I pretend aren't in the house, little spur of the moment gifts I sometimes buy for friends. Indulgent things. Things of pleasure and surprise.

TAPAS BAR
by Steve Bucher

We sat at the bar
Late spring
Eating tapas
Drinking barrel-aged gin
Tonic hinting orange
And undaunted thyme

We shared our lives
Sampling small plates of Boquerones

We touched our loves
Sipping blends of Amontillado and Cava

We limned our losses
In hour fallen absent
And obscure

You were married
I nearly so

Tète a tète
Over small plates of squid
Sausage
And flavors barrel-aged

No star to fix the night

A tear draped your cheek
I reached across
We kissed

Barrel-aged herbs
Gin potatoes
Cured olives and Manchego

THE WAY TO MY HEART

We left the tapas bar
For separate homes
Separate shores
Not knowing when
Or if

Lost to months
Oceans distant
We shared mornings for nights
Barrel-aged memories
Of tapas
Holding hands
A kiss

We staked a winter path
Through biting rock and thorn
Remembering small plates of squid
And sausage
Chilled drinks
Barrel-aged

Desolate
We held distant hands
Absorbing the bitter bleak

Pain like piety
Barrel-aged pain
On small plates

I lifted you
You lifted me

Across seas
Across moons
Across small plates
And glasses chilled

A, YOUR NAME IS ANNA
by Sheila Wellehan

Eating an apple is a commitment.
It demands more work than other fruit.

You must bite harder
and chew with more vigor,
respect ritual and history.

Tradition dictates a thorough visual inspection
to avoid consuming someone else's home.

Then buff the apple's skin
until it's shining.
Admire your efforts before the best part.

Hold its stem firmly
and twist clockwise gently,
one alphabet letter for each turn around—

A, your name is Anna
B, your name is Ben

remember chanting names,
your history of true loves and crushes,
study the faces in that long parade.

Smile at childhood cheating—
pulling stems up hard to land on the right letter,
faking twists to slow fate down.

Feel how deeply you trusted apples
to reveal the first name
of your future husband or wife.

FRIED CLAMS WITH A SIDE OF ONION RINGS
by Lucia Cherciu

A boring date used to be like eating a peanut butter
and jelly sandwich for lunch. I hate
peanut butter and jelly sandwiches
and I don't understand how they work.
Why would I want to eat anything
that tastes like sugar on sugar?
Just the thought makes me gag.
Why would I miss the call for a real lunch?

What I really want is the salt
and the crunch of falling in love.

Loving you is like ordering
fried clams with a side of onion rings
when we're sitting together
at a restaurant on the peer
while the waves crash against the boards
and three pelicans sit for a picture,
peck their feathers,
and dive for fish.
I dip the fried clams
into the horseradish sauce
and count on my tongue
a hundred secrets I adore about you
and don't need to spell out.

WEATHER REPORT
by Gretchen Fletcher

The space above the restaurant table separating them seemed to crackle with sparks. She was never one to raise her voice in thunderous anger, but she could shoot lightning bolts from her eyes. Right now she wished she could shoot bullets. How could he? To be so stupid as to get sucked into that game with the native and his match sticks and lose all their vacation money! She decided not to say anything. She would just stare at him all through dinner. And she wouldn't talk to him in their room after that either.

"What's the matter, hon?" he asked.

Look at his stupid, big, round, baby face, she thought. Mr. Innocent. That guy in the red and yellow and green knit cap must have seen him coming. Sucker from the States, he probably thought.

She looked out the window of the second-floor restaurant to the patio below. She could see the umbrella-topped table where that afternoon he had downed too many rum punches in the hot sun and started playing that match stick game.

It was obvious the guy had a trick. Even she could see that. But, no, Mr. Gullible had to keep on, thinking he could figure out the secret and win all his money back. Now they were stuck here in Virgin Gorda in the British Virgin Islands with no cash and a credit card dangerously close to maxed out.

And to top it all off, there was thunder rumbling in the distance. There was probably a storm coming, and now they wouldn't even be able to lie on the beach tomorrow.

At least she thought she had heard thunder. The restaurant was playing Vivaldi's "Four Seasons" on their sound system over and over. As soon as "Winter" ended, "Spring" started again. On some kind of looped tape, she thought. Like her life with him. Over and over. On and on. The music was so loud it drowned out everything else in the restaurant. Not that there was much to hear.

There were only two other tables of people talking quietly. And there certainly wasn't going to be any conversation at their table. She would see to that.

"Look at that! Above those people's table. A rat! Running across the rafters. Boy! You see everything in the islands. And this is a nice place, too."

She hated herself for looking where he was pointing. It was a rat! Ye gods! What next? She didn't give him the satisfaction of a comment on the rat.

As she watched it run across the rafters to the strains of "Autumn," a flash of eerie green light flooded the restaurant. A few seconds later, thunder cracked. How do you figure out how far away a storm is? She couldn't remember. Something about One Mississippi, Two Mississippi. He would know. But, no, I won't give him the satisfaction of asking him.

The waiter came with their entrees. At least while we're eating I won't have to talk, she reasoned. She stabbed her steak with a vengeance meant for him.

The next crack of thunder was followed too closely by its accompanying flash of lightning. Didn't that mean the storm was almost over them? She looked out at the marina beside the patio where he had lost all their money that afternoon. The masts of the sail boats docked there were leaning at crazy angles, blown by the wind bringing the storm. Halyards clanged rhythmically against aluminum masts.

Crrrack! This time the sound and light were almost simultaneous. She looked out as a big gust of wind picked the umbrella partway out of its slot in the table and dropped it over on its side. A plastic chair scooted across the patio and fell into the pool.

Then the Vivaldi stopped. It was very quiet.

"They've lost their power! It's a good thing they already cooked our dinners," he said cheerily. She could see his big, stupid face in the candlelight. It looked sweet. And safe. She gave him a small smile. Maybe he wouldn't be able to see it in the dim light of the candle.

She reached for the salt just as he did. He patted her hand as he relinquished the shaker to her. Ever the gentleman, she thought. After she salted her baked potato she passed the shaker to him, making sure that their hands met again.

"Thanks, hon. Say, this is fun, isn't it? Kind of cozy, don't you think?" he said just as the rain started to lash against the window in sheets.

"Yeah, I guess so," she answered in spite of her resolve. "But how are we ever going to get back across the patio to our room?"

"We'll make it. Just like we'll make it through our vacation. We'll just be careful about what we charge. And I didn't tell you, but I packed some traveler's checks in the pocket of your suitcase just in case we needed some extra cash while we were down here."

The thunder and lightning had let up by the time they left the restaurant. It was still raining, but their room was just across the patio. He took off his jacket and put it over her head, then scooped her up in his arms and ran for their room.

She was laughing in spite of herself when he put her down on the bed and flopped down next to her. His jacket was soaked, as was her hair, which stuck to her face in long, wet strips. She sucked on the one that had spread across her mouth. He took it out of her mouth and put it in his.

I CAME FROM THE VILLAGE OF PAINTED TOENAILS, YOU CAME FROM THE VILLAGE OF SHAVING CREAM
by Dianna Henning

Your mouth hugged my mouth
as though it were a plum.
The stars outside our tent rankled
for better seats. *Intruder*, you yelled,
and zipped the flap. Your sleeping-bag
inched into a cocoon. The moon as it pressed
through nylon spread silver on our lips.

My heart fished for trout when you
whispered my salty name. We could
have made our home anywhere—a good
ground-cover, an oiled skillet, but you were
the man from Shaving Cream Village, and I
was the woman with a penchant for fancy toes.

We dipped into the river and let our fish go.

KITCHEN NOTE: SEVERE SEAFOOD ALLERGY, SEAT 2
by Emily O'Neill

at dinner with Nai I ate a fried clam
when I kissed you hours later
you didn't die / the mouth is sometimes a liar

or scrubbed clean
by liquor / consider the oyster
the way it was intended / snapped shut

around a polished accident / there are rooms
we cannot enter / I've stopped
accepting sips of shell / started living on a chain

same last name as the dead drunk
playwright & still no one can spell it / same as
everybody dropping in a second R where it won't belong

take me to the desert instead of the beach
mescal in little clay pots / call it
cactus vodka / nothing will harm you here

harmonica, a joke towards borrowed time
we miss meals / stories & cigarettes ruin
me / strange condition / if I could have anything for dinner

wouldn't I ask you to choose / more jokes to borrow
more time / keep my hair pinned back / ask to split
the check / concern a kind of fear

tattoo me with oyster pearls / side of me
you can't touch without swelling
getting out of bed isn't anyone's feast

MAN-HANDS
by Autumn Konopka

I.
The family hands are thick.
I know. I have them.
Man-hands,

meaty and rough-knuckled,
that have shamelessly scrubbed
other people's toilets,
cradled children too soon, in birth
and death,
and thrown the first fistful of dirt
over too many unworthy husbands.

II.
I roll the dough for the cookies
on the kitchen counter
with the marble rolling pin.
Grandmother. Mother. Self.
Three generations.
Thick hands
tying paper-thin dough into delicate knots,
frying that fabric,
dressing it with powdered sugar.
The same hands
working different rites
in the tradition.

When you enter here,
it is the only time you will
hear me say, "This is woman's work,"
as I sit you at the table,
to watch
the sweat slowly simmering on my brow
from the force of rolling dough
with the whole body.

III.
I have loved your whole body
with mine, with hard hands that become
delicate
inside the span of your wide palm.

Tonight, linger
after kneading loose the tight dough of my shoulders.
Your cracking sandpaper knuckles,
the toothy saws of your habit-chewed fingernails,
with just that touch
will make me hum.
Listen: This is my song,
the song of my hopeful mother, and hers before
our hands grew callused
from pushing so many men away.

LEMON
by Emily Weitzman

Eat a lemon. Lemons are sour and you love them.
Suck on it until all the juice is gone and your teeth are falling out
No one will want to kiss you once your teeth have fallen out
Write about what this feels like, for no one to want to kiss you
How it is the same as being an apple core stuck in the kitchen sink.

Next, dress yourself in tomatoes.
Everyone knows that tomatoes are sexy.
Walk around like a sexy tomato.
Do not write about the moment when he looks at you
Write about the moment he walks past and doesn't look back.

Run to your bed, you sexy tomato.
Cry tears of artichokes.
Lay in a pile of your artichoke tears.
Allow the pile to grow, until you can swim in your artichoke tears
Do the breaststroke through the green water.
Build yourself a float—do not let him build it for you
Write about what it feels like using your own hands to build a float
Do not write about his hands.

Drift down the river—as far as your artichoke tears will take you.
Keep your eyes closed, so you can't know if he is watching
Do not wonder if you have floated to his back door
Do not pray that he will only see you covered in yourself
Write in the dark, as sun after sun must be rising in front of you.

Do not write about the sunrise.
Write about the kale, how you feel it growing from the surrounding earth
How it is beginning to get caught in your toes.
Write about what the kale might mean
Or what the kale can't mean
Or what you want the kale to mean.
Only stop writing months later, once even your hair is covered in kale.

THE WAY TO MY HEART

Let yourself sit through the years, surrounded, without ever swallowing.

Open your eyes suddenly.
Start writing all the beauty you see
If you see no beauty, write it into existence
Be surprised that you are not surprised at whatever is in front of you
Whether it be an avocado or a mountain
A rooftop or a strawberry
Him or not him
Take it all in.
Stare with your eyes like that's all they can do.

When something stares back—be it strawberry or him
Stop staring and move.
Write as you dance through the soil
Your legs your only instrument
Trace with your heel:
Everything that happens, happens again
Reach your toes toward the distance
And play hopscotch on the vegetables.
If you step on an olive, eat it, of course.
Never pass up a good olive
But thank the olive first.

Then run back
Run with the olive in your mouth
Back through the soil and strawberries and rooftops and kale
And back through the years of sunset after sunset
And if the float that you built is broken, swim up against the current
And unripen those artichoke tears, you sexy tomato
The sink needs to be drained and no one wants to kiss you
And it's time to reach back to the lemon.

Lemons are sour and you love them.

EXHIBITION EATER
by Brandon French

I grew up in a family that worshipped God in the temple, but food at home. They were scandalized when a cousin by marriage, a heathen named Marlene, laid out five slices of cheese for four people and concluded, when they were too polite to take the last slice, that she had served too much.

This same Marlene invited my parents and me to dinner and set out four small bowls of soup. That was it! Soup! And it wasn't a thick soup with lots of chicken or beef and dumplings. It was more like a broth. We sat at the table drumming our fingers and waiting for the next course for almost an hour until Marlene served dessert. Five cookies, and they weren't even chocolate chip, just some stale gingersnaps which tasted like dog kibble. Marlene finally ate the fifth one so we didn't have to worry about being impolite.

But even though the adults in my family were food worshippers (with the exception of Marlene), my kid cousins were finicky eaters. They liked their hotdogs with *ketchup*! And they thought mustard, even the yellow French's kind, was the condiment of death. And if anybody tried to force something like *chopped liver* on them, they'd hide under the table or retch their way to the bathroom with a chorus of ewws, arrrghs, ughhs, and brfffs.

I, on the other hand, *loved* chopped liver. I even liked *raw oysters* (so long as they were loaded with cocktail sauce). That's how I became the family's exhibition eater, starting when I was four.

"Look at Jamie. She eats everything!" That's what they'd tell their kids, which didn't exactly endear me to my cousins, who thought I was just showing off.

I also liked bones. Give me a bone and I was busy for an hour, especially if it was a lamb leg bone, or a roast beef bone, or a Porterhouse steak bone, although I could polish off one of those in half the time. I also liked chicken bones, which I cracked open with my teeth so I could suck out the marrow.

"I hope you won't do that in a restaurant, or when you go out on a date, Jamie," my dad would say, although at the age of four, I thought it was a moot point.

But I knew he was proud of the way I ate because it was a status symbol in our family to have a kid like me and he didn't have a lot of status at the time, being a mostly-unemployed musician. It was also something we had in common, like garlic or Worcestershire sauce, or roast duck, which was my absolute favorite.

You might be inclined to think that I was a fat kid, but judging from pictures, I was skinny until I became eight. At eight, I had a little belly and my cheeks were on the chubby side. That was around the time my parents got divorced, so I guess food became a consolation.

When I was in high school, I baked a devil's food cake with chocolate whipped cream icing and polished off the whole thing in less than two days. And once, when I was babysitting, I ate an entire canned ham, jelly and all, even though after the first few bites, it tasted like a salt lick. I remember hiding the can deep in the family's garbage pail so they wouldn't know what I'd done until they went looking for the ham, probably a long time later, I figured, and by then they wouldn't suspect me.

But in my senior year of high school, I decided I wanted to be popular, so I bleached my brown hair platinum blond and went on a diet. The boy I had my eye on was a sexy Italian guy named Joe Agozino who played pretend bongos on the school desks, and Joe liked skinny blondes. Once I became a skinny blonde, sure enough, Joe liked me. And he didn't even seem to mind that I was a *smart* blonde instead of a dumb one. He became my obsession, and I could hardly stand to eat. You could have waved a prime rib or a roast duck at me back then and I wouldn't have even blinked. All I wanted was Joe.

"How come you like me so much?" he'd ask.

"Because you're wonderful."

"What's so wonderful about me?"

"Everything."

"How come you won't let me French kiss you, then?"

That's where our relationship got rocky. According to Joe, all the *dumb* blondes French kissed. This was a long time ago, when French kissing was *verboten*, not like now, when "oral" isn't even considered sex. This was when girls who "went all the way" were called "tramps." Not that French kissing was "all the way." But it was definitely *on* the way, and at the time it seemed to me like a slippery slope.

So Joe and I broke up. And that's when I started to eat again. There was a big empty space in me that Joe had filled, and food was the only other way I knew how to handle it. Joe was my first *badass*, although back then we called them *hoods*, short for hoodlum. But he wasn't really a *hood*, just a sweet, horny teenager who joined the Army after he graduated from high school and was killed in a helicopter crash on his way to Hanau Army Airfield in Hessen, Germany. After I heard about that, I was really sorry that I hadn't French kissed him. I hope a whole lot of other girls did.

That summer, I made a lot of secret trips in my mother's Chevrolet to the Donut Depot, pretending for the counter boy's benefit that there were several other people out in the car waiting for doughnuts .

"Okay, Jane wants two glazed, and Henry wants an old fashioned and a maple bar. Let me see, I think Terry said he wanted a bear claw, and Tony definitely asked for two chocolate-with-sprinkles. How many is that? Seven? Okay then, just give me two chocolate bars, an apple fritter, and . . . two glazed twists."

Back in the car, I'd eat the whole dozen and they wouldn't even fill me up. Food can get tricky when you start eating for all the wrong reasons.

At college, I got skinny again because the cafeteria food at the dorm was grotty, and there was this boy—Dolph.

"Is that short for Dolphin?

"No, Adolph."

"As in Hitler?"

"He spelled it differently."

I didn't have the heart to correct him.

Dolph was a tall, blond, sun-bronzed surfer boy from Malibu, California, and just walking next to him made me feel proud. So I went on the black coffee diet, ten or twelve cups a day, and got really skinny. We did just great with each other for a couple of weeks, rolling around on his bed in the fraternity house kissing and *almost* "doing it." But then we completely ran out of anything to say to each other. I mean nothing, not one word. So I had to admit to myself that the most beautiful boy in the world was totally boring. And that, as they say, was that.

My weight continued to go the way of my love life: up when I was unattached, down when I had a beau. In New York, after I graduated from college, I had my first major relationship, with a crazy minimalist painter named Georg who made me so insecure, I became anorexic.

"You see that boat, Jamie? That's how I'm going to leave you," he'd say.

"Don't say that, Georg. You're making me cry."

"You see that girl, the pretty one in the halter top with the blond ponytail? That's who I'm going to leave you for."

"Georg, stop! Do you want me to kill myself?"

He got up to 200 pounds during the three years we were together and I dropped down to 89, living on chocolate bars, malted milk, and a steak every three or four days at Max's Kansas City, which I had to split with Georg because we were poor. I wrote down every detail of our tortured relationship in tiny printed letters like a medieval monk's manuscript, three journals' worth, until the last entry said, "I am pregnant."

For the next nine months I ate enormous breakfasts of bacon and eggs and toast dripping with butter, and lots of cold milk. And for dinner I had a huge carton of pork fried rice from one of the best Sechuan restaurants in Chinatown. Still, I only weighed 104 pounds the day after I gave birth.

Georg was amazed that he had made a baby and he tried to be a good father, but it just wasn't in him. He eventually left me and Gunther for a sculptor who made plaster knots that looked like elephant snot.

My weight has been up and down since then, except for the time when my vodka and chardonnay diet took me way up and kept me there for most of a decade. But lately, after losing 25 pounds, I've become the exhibition eater for Weightwatchers.

"Look here," I say, mixing a small amount of yogurt and dill dressing into a baby kale salad with a four ounce side of water-packed canned salmon. "A delicious, filling, vegetable and protein lunch that's only six points out of the 30-point daily allowance."

And there isn't even a man in my life as an incentive, I'm proud to say, although I always keep my eye out for one.

AUBADE
by Katherine Anderson Howell

Cynthia, is it strange
that I woke tasting
your pavlova this morning?
Crisp meringue and cream
on my tongue.

I remember the way you
carried it gently
into my house,
shared the ritual
of pomegranate seeds
with only me.

You left on your bike,
your cello strapped
to the back.
Like most dark
nights in Cambridge,
old leaves slicked
the brick sidewalks.
I waved, shouted "Be careful,"
stepped back into the light.

Then in October
Lisa's voice cracked over
memorial service,
diary, please
don't tell.

And all I think
is pavlova, round white,
an open pomegranate spilling
over the top.

Cynthia, forgive me all
I can't mourn.

FIRST FALL FROST
by Brenda Yates

Cowboy boots in New England? Bell bottoms.
Tangled hair cascading onto a lace shirt. Star-
light glints on your gold-rim glasses; walrus

mustache shadows your smile. You point out
constellations, speaking without our familiar
flattened vowels. Karen and I hug ourselves,

impatient in Capezios and mini-skirts. It's late,
night turned cold and the lift you needed miles
out of our way. Down a bumpy road between

ripening apple orchards, their sweet smell over-
whelms even the too-crisp air. I turn to protest,
listening for a place to break in; words continue

to tumble from your hidden mouth. I count four
I've never heard, tilt and whirl into a star map
of mythology, physics, and astronomy. Inviting

us in, you warm us with hot cider and feed us
apple cake. Driving home, both Karen and I
wonder aloud why I'd agreed to lunch. You're

skinny, not very tall, and lack the muscular grace
of jocks I date. At lunch you talk, you listen; we
stroll by the river. Your kiss, your skin have

the scent of apples. I tilt and whirl, moving in
that night. Forty-odd autumns later, a soft snore
wakes me. On your sleeping face, a now white

mustache shines in silvery moonlight, your round
cheeks and rounder face replacing those once
angular lines. I push and you stir. We turn, your

familiar arm finding its place between my breasts, tucking under my jaw. And a scent of apples as I tilt toward sleep.

BREAKFAST AT POMPEII
by Susan J. Erickson

Some lovers breakfast on figs, plump
and purple, on sun-succulent peaches
or crescent moon slices of melon
but you fed me golden popovers

created in those ash-clouded hours
while I dreamt I could foresee the landscape
of my future. The molten silk
of flour, milk, eggs, butter, and salt

erupted like volcanoes we devoured
in the then and there, diverting
the flow of time like the marmalade
rivulets streaming down our fingers.

Like lovers at Pompeii,
caught in natural consequences,
those lost mornings on the rim of fire
are cast in stone.

NOTE ON THE REFRIGERATOR
by Sharon Lask Munson

I've made
rice pudding
for your birthday

your favorite—
thick, smooth
studded with dark raisins

slow-baked
to a golden custard.

Indulge me,
always
the missing spoonful.

SWEETNESS
by Caroline Bock

One bite, that's what I offer Louise.

The idiot doctor had said I should go home and get some rest. I don't know when I slept last—weeks ago, before her diagnosis.

She'll have a bite, and then I'll finish it, even though I'm a guy who before I met her would tell you: I don't like sweets. The dessert is in my hand, and my hand is near her lips, and she must smell the vapors of sugar; she must know I'm here. Dusting powder falls like snow or cocaine on my work shirt.

I hadn't been with Louise long, just over a year, long enough to not want to sleep without her. We weren't old when we first met; she was just past thirty. Some people think that's still young, but she didn't.

She was a girl with curves, that's what I thought the first time I saw her through the open door of the Raven Grill, and then inside, next to me, asking for directions. She was, I mean, she is Italian; she'd say Sicilian, from a village in the mountains outside Palermo, a place we will visit some day she said that first night. She was saying this and feeding me bits of *pignoli*, almonds and pine nuts and butter in a cookie, and I was thinking: you must have been born smelling sweet. We were only going together a couple of weeks before we got married at City Hall. I soon learned that she swooned over *sfogliatelle*, *struffoli*, *tiramisu*. I fumbled with the consonants and vowels in these desserts, maybe even bumbling them on purpose because it made her laugh. She liked to buy these treats from the old-time bakery next to the hipster coffee shop, the bakery that couldn't be bought out when the neighborhood changed, the bakery that still puts your desserts in a cardboard box and pulls down a red and white string from a hive of strings and ties it all up with a double knot. She must have felt like a queen bee swinging those boxes into our apartment on a Friday night. She'd make pasta—*don't say spaghetti*, she'd say—and I'd say, *oh, oh, spa-get-tio-s* just so she'd get mad, fake mad, and pour us another class of dark red wine and swing her hips.

Louise never went as far as singing opera, but in my dreams she did. I spent my whole life listening to rock and punk, and in my dreams when I slept beside her, I heard arias. She never wanted to go out on Friday nights. I spent the years before Louise at happy hours drinking two-for-one beers and snatching at greasy sliders and wings, suffering the indignities of compulsively checking my phone, as if I had plans, as if someone or something important was coming my way, nothing did until her, and suddenly on Fridays I was skipping lunch, working out at the gym, going home taut and hungry. The rest of the workweek we'd stay late at our respected jobs. Afterwards, we'd meet for something quick, a salad for her, a burger for me. Now on Fridays, I was home drinking wine, eating pasta with homemade sauce, a *biscotti* or *pizzelle* or *tartufo,* to end the meal, *to end the week with sweetness,* she'd say. Her lips swathed in powdered sugar, we'd make love and count crumbs in the dwell of her cleavage, and make more love. And plans. We had plans for that trip to Sicily next fall. Hustling down drugs, which are legal in California and Oregon to kill my sweetheart, collapsed with *gliobastoma multiforme,* that reeks, that's foul-tasting, that there's no playing around with pronouncing, that means: brain tumor.

    Her dark hair weaves against the white sheets.

    Her dark eyes open, and weep.

    "One last bite," I say. "You'll only taste the cream of the cannoli. You'll only taste the sugar. And then I'll take a bite, and—" These words heave out of me; my hand shudders, what I taste is chalky and dusty, the world, spinning and buzzing, even though nothing has touched my lips.

    All of her refuses me. Instead, she eases over, doing her best to hide the pain in her bones. I throw away the tainted dessert, scrub my hands, and crawl into bed beside her. She brings the fingers that would have fed her poison to her lips, as if this is the pact: we will both suffer, but not alone, not yet. And I kiss her mouth, and I find the reigning hollow of her sunken breasts, and I sleep.

THE FLAVOR OF SEPTEMBER
by Pamela Murray Winters

I'm the one who gathers the thyme, the sage,
the savory. You rub it in your hard hands,

and I remember Neruda: *love…milled us
to a single flour.* That's how flavor works,

except in curry, where each spice is time-
release, blossoming on the tongue, surprise

after surprise. You tell me some of what
you need. Kitchen scissors. That jar of rice.

I never knew you for a chef, so this
afternoon is a surprise. A gift. We eat

outside, forkfuls of tender chicken,
our eyes on eyes, not mouths, our ears

full of the calls of the creatures, changing
their voices, quivering in the trees.

MERMAID IN THE KITCHEN
by John C. Mannone

Her palace, wallpapered with corals and shells, is filled with glistening pearls, spills with amber light. By the window, the kitchen table is anchored—fashioned from a sunken sailboat deck with teakwood planks.

Field greens topped with blue cornflowers—blue as the Mediterranean and drizzled with vinaigrette—cover the aquarium-clear dish. A small trident fork lies next to it, and a crystal goblet of beer effervesces.

Blue mussels, in white wine & chicken stock, steam scents of fenugreek and saffron. She garnishes with parsley. For him, she grills wild swordfish on live oak coals, basted with olive oil, lemon juice, capers, thyme, and a hint of anchovy paste. She will not eat the fish, but would the buttered peas and potatoes, and the wood-grilled squash.

With each morsel her prince eats, she listens to him beg for stories of storms, of ships lost, and of deep-sea wonders that she had seen. And of the sea witch, who likes to lace the ale with her own black blood. (It wasn't to wash the seaweed down.) She tells him when—before the sun would rise—and how she had to swim to shore with that brew in hand, sit on the rocks, then swallow the fiery bitter draught. She watched her own tail split and transform into shapely human legs.

He is sweating now. So she serves him a sea breeze of exotic fruits: mangos, pineapple, apricots, peaches, oranges, strawberries, too, tossed with a little sugar, cinanamon and brandy, served over vanilla ice cream in a scalloped dish.

Outside her kitchen-palace, she grows an expansive garden full of crimson red and deep blue trees. Their fruits glitter like golden apples, and their blossoms flame like fire on their constantly waving stalks.

MORMON AND JEW: A ROMANCE IN FOOD
by Felicia Rose

Felicia

It's a mild July afternoon. I could be strolling along the river in our northern Utah town or sitting on the porch reading May Swenson poems. Instead, I'm laboring in the kitchen freezing and drying sixty pounds of cherries. Why? Because cherry season is on, and according to my wife, Monte, who orchestrates such tasks, "Our food storage has become dangerously low."

I know what she means. The quarter cow we received in December has dwindled to a mere one fifth, the venison jerky is slowly disappearing, and the trout is six pounds away from gone. In our cellar pantry, the size of a New York apartment, an entire shelf lies bare.

"Should the Apocalypse hit," she says, "mark my word, we'll be happy we have it."

Ladle in hand, I scoop cherries and nod.

"I come by it honestly," she adds, her expression one of unease. "Look at how my parents live." How can I miss it? True to their Mormon pioneer heritage, buckets of wheat and beans and corn cover two basement walls; storage freezers, packed to the brim, line the third. Boxes and cans and jars peek out of cupboards and from beneath tables and beds. Open the closet and be greeted by barrels of oats. This is a land where people haul truckloads of potatoes from Idaho and buy cans by the case.

Monte

Everyone knows Jews are neurotic, and New York Jews the most. But my Felicia elevates the art of neurosis to wedding-cake heights.

Take, for instance, the way she packs my lunch. Rain or shine, sleet or hail, fever or fight, by 7:00 a.m. my lunchbox sits on the counter, ready to escort me to work. It eases my mornings, and I adore her for that. But come noon, the challenge begins. To free the fruit from the tin, I must summon the techniques of Houdini. Why does she screw the lid on so tight? What's the risk my compote will flee? Then there are the rubber bands. On good days we have two on each half sandwich, on bad days three or four. Why? So that the waxed paper, folded in complex origami, does not come undone. "Has any victual or libation ever sullied your lunchbox?" she asks. She has a point. The innards of my lunchbox remain as pure as my love.

Felicia

What we now call salad comes from the Latin *sal* meaning salt. And to my mind, that's what a salad contains. So the first time my in-laws ask us to bring a salad for lunch, I toss arugula and cress with oil and salt. "It's lovely," Monte says. "But I doubt anyone'll eat it." This is how I learn that in Mormon Utah "salad" means chunks of canned pineapple mixed with Cool Whip and lime-flavored Jell-O. I start again. For good measure, I toss in a pinch of salt.

Monte

I hated attending religious services as a child. The preaching maddened me. The rituals irked me. I wanted to be in the canyon playing hunter and gatherer or in the orchards eating a peach. Not Felicia.

"I liked attending synagogue," she says. "In our small Brooklyn congregation, I was the only child among elderly Jews."

I picture five-year-old Felicia, dark ponytail extending from a floral babushka, swaying in prayer among dozens of white-bearded men and a handful of women.

"Weren't you bored?" I ask.

"Not really. I knew that afterward there'd be a buffet of herring and onions and challah."

My wife has curious taste. I shouldn't be surprised. After all, she chose me.

Felicia

Monte's eyes betray an impish expression. "It was the raccoon's fault," she says.

"The raccoon?"

"Remember I told you about our pet raccoon? The one we drove home on the top of the car."

"Oh, that raccoon." I envision little Monte, long yellow hair tied in a braid, feeding potato chips to the raccoon through the car window.

"As a child, I'd hide food in the closet for Fast Sunday. One time, the raccoon escaped from its cage and ate my marshmallows. I had nothing else to eat."

The moral of this story? I'm married to someone who considers marshmallows food.

The other moral of the story? I'm married to an imp. And it pleases me to no end that I am.

Monte

Felicia has good taste in books. And for the most part, even her musical choices pass muster. But to put it mildly, some of her food is disgusting. Consider her fondness for fish. I'm not referring to civilized fish, a filleted piece of salmon or trout. No. I'm referring to the kind that reeks even before she opens the can. And when she does, beware. Those scaly creatures, sardines she calls them, look as though they might awaken, headless though they are, but not tailless, skinless or boneless, and swim out of their oily can. "Do you actually enjoy those?" I ask from across the kitchen. "Or do you just eat them for health?"

"They're yummy," she replies.

It's high time I introduce her to pork.

Felicia

The seventy-two-hour emergency kit has its perks. Ample and tidy, this Mormon directive contains much one might need should a band of marauders come along and insist we join them at once. Still, its contents lack many a staple. Where, for instance, are the bialys? The brisket? The borscht? I see no reason for these crucial omissions. And the flashlight. In the same bag as the food! If the batteries leak, we'll die. Better to eat in the dark.

"You have a point," Monte says. She replaces the flashlight with matches and candles.

"That's more like it, my dear." Now the seventy-two-hour kit doubles as a picnic basket. Summer evenings we dine on the porch, candles flickering in wine glasses, our dessert a lingering kiss.

Monte

Felicia is in heaven. She closes her eyes and a look of ecstasy appears on her face. Before her sits a chunk of gefilte fish floating in jelly. "Wanna try some?" she asks.

It resembles a dried piece of loofah. "Maybe not, but I'd be happy to massage you with it."

"How about a smidgeon of aspic?" She teases my lips with a spoon. "Just close your eyes and think of Jell-O."

Truth be told, the texture is surprisingly pleasant.

Felicia

Some years ago, I came across a recipe for funeral potatoes. The chef, a Utah native, had attended cooking school in New York and had gotten ideas. To the eighteen or twenty potatoes in cream sauce he added a minced clove of garlic.

Intrigued by the recipe, I surprise Monte for our anniversary dinner with this unorthodox version of Mormon comfort food. "It's very good," she says. "Actually, it's quite tasty." Her expression suggests alertness, a hint of confusion though not of distaste.

"But..?" I ask.

"But I'm wondering if you added some garlic."

"You know, my dear, I've been meaning to place a pea under our mattress. Then again, you're already my princess."

Monte

Before I met Felicia, I knew about kosher only from pickles. But there's more to it than that. Take chickens, for instance. It's not enough to buy a kosher chicken. One needs to kosher it further at home. Why? "If for no other reason," says Felicia, "it tastes better that way."

So here I am, a *shikse* standing at the kitchen counter on a Friday afternoon massaging salt into the cavity of a hen.

And what does Felicia say? "I'm sure looking forward to dinner."

MELDING
by Bryn Homuth
For J

I watch as my wife slices peaches,
knife slipped under outer membrane
to peel back molten skin,
a small model of the sun
turning on its axis
in her hand, plasmatic flesh
like a star enclosed in her fingers.
She divides one into quarters,
the blade's bump on pit,
a brown, wicker-like lattice buried
in flesh. Red-tipped wedges drop
into the bowl; she fishes
out a slippery piece, extends it
to me, fingers brushing cheek and lip.
The fruit dissolves on my tongue
while I measure flour,
counter dusted patchy white
like an early snowfall.
She pours macerated peaches
into a baking dish, lava-like.
Once in the oven, heat weds
wet and dry, sugar melts
to thick syrup, caramelized
corners bubble and blend.
While the cobbler cools, we lean
against the refrigerator,
its hum at my back,
my wife resting her head
on my shoulder, drawing
my arms across her front,
fitting to my embrace.

CONTRIBUTOR BIOGRAPHIES

Lynn Abendroth is a NC native who is now a happy San Francisco resident. She earned a BA and MFA from Mills College and has been previously published in *The Andersen Anthology* and the *Journal of the San Francisco Medical Society*.

Jessica Abughattas is an MFA candidate at Antioch University. Her poems appear in *THRUSH Poetry Journal*, *Heavy Feather Review*, *Roanoke Review*, and elsewhere.

Susan McGee Bailey directed the Wellesley Centers for Women and served as a professor Women & Gender Studies and Education at Wellesley College for twenty-five years. She retired to spend more time with her developmentally and physically challenged daughter and to work on a memoir, *The Evolution of a Feminist*, which braids the past fifty years of U.S. feminism with her experience as a single mother. Susan's non-academic writing has appeared in *MS Magazine*, *The Boston Globe*, and on the *Brevity* Blog.

Caroline Bock is the author of the critically acclaimed young adult novels *Lie* and *Before My Eyes* (St. Martin's Press). She dedicates her short story to the memory of her mother, Louise (née Garofalo) Blech, who loved all things sweet.

Steve Bucher lives and writes poetry in the Virginia Piedmont. He is an active member of the Poetry Society of Virginia. Steve's poetry appears in such places as *Blue Heron Review*, *Artemis Journal*, *California Quarterly*, *deLuge Journal*, and *NoVA Bards*.

Lucia Cherciu is a Professor of English at SUNY/Dutchess in Poughkeepsie, NY, and she writes both in English and in Romanian. Her books include *Train Ride to Bucharest* (Sheep Meadow Press), *Edible Flowers* (Main Street Rag), *Lepădarea de Limbă/The Abandonment of Language* (Vinea), and *Altoiul Râsului/Grafted Laughter* (Brumar). Her poetry was nominated twice for a Pushcart Prize and Best of the Net.

Steve Cushman has published three novels and two poetry collections. He currently works at Cone Health in Greensboro, North Carolina.

Teresa De La Cruz earned her BA and MA in Creative Writing from San Francisco State University. Her poems have recently been featured on *PUBLIC POOL* and *Yellow Chair Review*, and a collection of her work can be found in the Rare Books vault of the U.S. Library of Congress. She is married to a wonderful chef and especially loves the San Jose Sharks, Bon Iver, Iceland, and wine.

Joanie DiMartino has had work published in many literary journals and anthologies, including *Modern Haiku*, *Alimentum*, *Calyx*, and *Circe's Lament: An Anthology of Wild Women*. She is a past winner of the Betty Gabehart Award for Poetry. DiMartino is the author of two collections of poetry, *Licking the Spoon* and *Strange Girls*, and is completing her third manuscript, *Wood to Skin*, about the 19th-century whaling industry, for which she was a 38th Voyager on the *Charles W. Morgan*.

Katherine Edgren's book *The Grain Beneath the Gloss*, published by Finishing Line Press, will be available soon. She also has two chapbooks: *Long Division* and *Transports*. Her poems have appeared in *Christian Science Monitor*, *Birmingham Poetry Review*, and *Barbaric Yawp*.

Jo Angela Edwins teaches writing and literature at Francis Marion University in Florence, SC. Her poems have appeared in various journals and anthologies, and her chapbook *Play* was published by Finishing Line Press in 2016. She is the 2014 recipient of the Carrie McCray Nickens Fellowship Prize in Poetry from the South Carolina Academy of Authors.

Terri Elders, a lifelong writer and editor, has been published in over a hundred anthologies. A native Californian, she earned an MSW from UCLA. After decades of working all over the world, she's happy as a clam to have returned to the Southland.

Susan J. Erickson's first full-length collection of poems, *Lauren Bacall Shares a Limousine*, won the Brick Road Poetry Prize. Her poems appear in *Crab Creek Review, The Fourth River, Terrain* and *The Tishman Review*. If she can't have popovers she'll take a flaky buttermilk biscuit.

Marta Ferguson is the co-editor of *Drawn to Marvel: Poems from the Comic Books* (Minor Arcana Press), the editor of the Columbia Art League's Interpretations anthology series, and the author of *Mustang Sally Pays Her Debt to Wilson Pickett* (Main Street Rag). Her poetry has appeared in dozens of literary magazines, including *The Cortland Review, Poet Lore, So to Speak,* and *Spillway*. A former poetry editor for *The Missouri Review*, Marta has been the sole proprietor of Wordhound Writing & Editing Services, LLC for 15 years.

Gretchen Fletcher was her husband's script writer as they travelled in Europe and the Caribbean producing travelogues for American Express and Trusthouse Forte Hotels. She has published travel articles in magazines and newspapers and produced two books of poetry. She won the Poetry Society of America's Bright Lights/Big City competition and read her winning poem in Times Square.

Brandon French has been an assistant professor of English at Yale, a published film scholar, a playwright and screenwriter, a psychoanalyst, and a mother. Forty-four of her stories have been accepted for publication by literary journals and anthologies, and she was an award winner in the 2015 Chicago Tribune Nelson Algren Short Story Contest.

Cameron D. Garriepy believes every day is your love story. She wrote her first romance novel in the eighth grade on an antique typewriter, using a stack of pink paper. Detours between that draft and publishing her first novel included a BA in Music from Middlebury College, a professional culinary education, and twelve years in the child-wrangling industry.

Dianna Henning holds an MFA in Writing '89 from Vermont College of Fine Arts. She has been published in places such as *Naugatuck River Review, Lullwater Review, The Red Rock Review,* and *The Kentucky Review*. Henning's third poetry book *Cathedral of the Hand* was published in 2016 by *Finishing Line Press*.

Misha Herwin is a writer of short stories and novels for adults and children. When she is not writing she loves to bake. Muffins are her specialty.

Lynn Hoffman is an artist and writer. He was born in Brooklyn, lives in Philadelphia, and is the author, most recently, of *Philadelphia Poems* and the romance novel *The Butterfly Farmer*.

Bryn Homuth is an adjunct English faculty member at Crown College, where he teaches introductory composition and literature. His poems have recently appeared in *The Tishman Review, The Turnip Truck(s),* and *Jabberwock Review,* among other print and online publications. Bryn's work has also been previously nominated for a Pushcart Prize and the *Best of the Net Anthology*.

Katherine Anderson Howell lives, writes, works, and parents in Washington, D.C. She writes in many genres, and her work can be found in *Gargoyle Magazine, The Rumpus, Pennsylvania English*, and the *Riveter Review*, among others.

Autumn Konopka is the author of the chapbook *a chain of paper dolls* (The Head & the Hand Press), and she was the 2016 poet laureate of Montgomery County, PA. Her poems have appeared in *Literary Mama, Crab Orchard Review, Birmingham Poetry Review, Philadelphia Stories*, and others.

John C. Mannone has work in *Blue Fifth Review, Peacock Journal, Gyroscope Review,* and *New England Journal of Medicine,* among other places. In addition to several nominations for Pushcart and Rhysling Awards, he's the recipient of the prestigious Jean Ritchie Fellowship (2017) for Appalachian writing; twice awarded a writing residency at Weymouth Center for the Arts & Humanities; has three poetry collections, including *Flux Lines* (Celtic Cat Publishing); and edits poetry for *Abyss & Apex* and other venues. He's a physicist raised in Baltimore, now living between Knoxville and Chattanooga, TN.

Peter Marcus's book *Dark Square* was published by Pleasure Boat Studio: A Literary Press. His poems have appeared in such places as *The Antioch Review, Boulevard, Crab Orchard Review,* and *Iowa Review*. He is the Off-Campus Academic Program Coordinator at Elms College Accelerated Bachelor's Degree in Psychology Programs at Holyoke and Mount Wachusetts Community Colleges.

Mary B. Moore's second full-length collection *Flicker*, Dogfish Head winner, and *Eating the Light*, Sable Books' chapbook award winner, appeared in 2016. Cleveland State published *The Book of Snow*. *Georgia Review*, *Poem/Memoir/Story*, *Cider Press Review*, and *Coal Hill Review* published recent poems, and work is forthcoming in *Nimrod*, where she won the Pablo Neruda Contest Second Place Award.

Alice Morris, a Minnesota native, comes to writing with a background in art, and she has been published in a West Virginia textbook and *The New York Art Review*. Her poems appear in *The Broadkill Review, Delaware Beach Life, Silver Birch Press*, and *The Avocet*, among other publications. Her poetry is also published or forthcoming in themed collections and anthologies, most recently, *Ice Cream Poems: reflections on life with ice cream, Rehoboth Reimagined,* and *Bared: Contemporary Poetry and Art on Bras and Breasts*.

Sharon Lask Munson is a poet, retired teacher, coffee addict, wine lover, and old movie enthusiast with many published poems, two chapbooks, and one full length book of poems. She lives and writes in Eugene, Oregon.

Emily O'Neill's debut collection, *Pelican*, is the inaugural winner of YesYes Books' Pamet River Prize for women and nonbinary writers and the winner of the 2016 Devil's Kitchen Reading Series. She is the author of three chapbooks: *Celeris* (Fog Machine), *You Can't Pick Your Genre* (Jellyfish Highway), and *Make a Fist & Tongue the Knuckles* (Nostrovia! Press). She teaches writing and tends bar in Boston, MA.

Chris Rodriguez is currently retired from conventional life, but is busy with her large garden and backyard chickens in Pocatello, ID. Her stories for children have appeared in *Cricket, Wee Wisdom*, and *R-A-D-A-R*. She is currently on fire with flash fiction, including work in Anthology Askew Volume 003 - *Askew Adventures* and several anthologies by Horrified Press.

Felicia Rose is a writer, editor and homesteader. She has published in *The Helicon West Anthology*, *The League of Utah Writers Anthology*, and various journals. When the spirit moves her, she pens essays and how-to articles for *Mother Earth News*.

Born in Manhattan, New York in the last year of the 1950's, **Miguel A. Rueda** grew up during the turbulent Sixties. The racial, political, and social upheavals of the next three decades shaped the way he viewed the world around him. Miguel has been published in numerous anthologies under his given name and his pen name, Wayne Hills.

Anna Schoenbach seems normal enough, but her true nature yearns to break free in a written form. She writes with a different perspective of the truth and, by the guiding light of a candle, desires to be a flare of understanding in the darkness of ignorance. Mostly, though, she just writes.

Eric Paul Shaffer is author of six poetry books, including *A Million-Dollar Bill*; *Lāhaina Noon*; *Portable Planet*; and *Living at the Monastery, Working in the Kitchen*. More than 450 of his poems appear in reviews in Australia, Canada, England, Ireland, New Zealand, Nicaragua, Scotland, Wales, and the USA. Shaffer lives on O'ahu and teaches at Honolulu Community College.

Judy Swann is a poet, essayist, editor, and bicycle commuter whose work has been published in many venues both in print and online. Her book, *We Are All Well: The Letters of Nora Hall* has given her great joy. She lives in Ithaca, NY.

Julia Tagliere is a freelance writer and editor whose work has appeared in *The Writer* and *Hay & Forage Grower* magazines and online at *Buzzle*; in various anthologies, including *Here in the Middle: Stories of Love, Loss, and Connection from the Ones Sandwiched in between*, *Candlesticks and Daggers: An Anthology of Mixed Genre Mysteries*, and in the juried photography and prose collection *Love + Lust*. Her short story, "Te Absolvo," was named Best Short Story in the 2015 William Faulkner Literary Competition. Julia currently resides in Maryland with her family, where she recently completed her M.A. in Fiction Writing at Johns Hopkins University.

Mary Ellen Talley's poems have most recently been published in *Kaleidoscope* and *Peacock Journal* as well as in recent anthologies, including *The Doll Collection, All We Can Hold: poems of motherhood,* and *Raising Lilly Ledbetter Women Poets Occupy the Workspace*. She worked for many years with words and children as a Speech-Language Pathologist (SLP) in Washington public schools.

Betsy Fogelman Tighe has published widely in small literary magazines, including *Rattle*; *TriQuarterly* 74, for which she was nominated for a Pushcart Prize; and *Verseweavers*, Number 14 and Fall 2015, for which she was awarded third prize in the New Poets and first prize in the Dueling Judges categories, respectively, by the Oregon Poetry Association. In 2016, she was a finalist for the Snake Nation Press Violet Reed Haas book prize. She serves happily, exhaustedly, as a teacher-librarian in a Portland, OR high school and is the devoted mother of two young adults.

Paulene Turner is a Sydney writer of short stories, novels, and short plays. She is currently working on a YA book series with several different historical settings. This is her first adventure in romantic fiction.

Rachel Voss is a high school English teacher living in Queens, New York. She graduated with a degree in Creative Writing and Literature from SUNY Purchase College. Her work has previously appeared in *The Ghazal Page, Hanging Loose Magazine, Unsplendid, 3Elements Review, Silver Birch Press,* and *Bodega Magazine,* among others.

Emily Weitzman writes artichokes and eats poems. As a 2014-2015 Thomas J. Watson Fellow, she traveled the world solo for a year, teaching, performing, writing, and collaborating with spoken word poetry communities in New Zealand, Australia, Nepal, India, Sri Lanka, Cambodia, Italy, and Ireland. A restless traveler and an English teacher, she attends the MFA program in Nonfiction at Columbia University.

Sheila Wellehan's poetry is featured in *The Fourth River, Off the Coast, Poetry East, Tinderbox Poetry Journal,* and many other journals and anthologies. She lives in Cape Elizabeth, Maine.

Pamela Murray Winters is a Maryland-based writer whose poems have appeared in *Gargoyle*, the *Gettysburg Review*, *Slipstream*, and the *Unrequited* anthology, among other publications. She is a recipient of a Maryland State Arts Council grant for her poetry. Her first book, *The Unbeckonable Bird*, will be published in 2018.

Brenda Yates is the Pushcart-nominated author of *Bodily Knowledge* (Tebot Bach) and a recipient of the Beyond Baroque Literary Arts Center Poetry Prize. Her reviews, interviews, and poems have featured in such places as *Chaparral; The Tishman Review; KPFK Radio 90.7 (Why Poetry); The American Journal of Poetry;* and journals in Ireland, the United Kingdom, Israel, China, and Australia.

THE WAY TO MY HEART

ABOUT THE EDITOR

Kelly Ann Jacobson is a novelist, poet, and editor who has published, or has contracted to be published, twenty-one books, including the novel *Cairo in White* and the poetry collection *I Have Conversations with You in My Dreams*. Under her pen name, Annabelle Jay, she writes young adult fiction. *The Way to My Heart* is Kelly's sixth anthology.

THE WAY TO MY HEART

66271790R10075

Made in the USA
Lexington, KY
08 August 2017